T0360374

SHIMANO

VANFORD
FAST FORWARD

NEW TO 2024 IS THE VANFORD FA SERIES, A REVOLUTIONARY ADVANCEMENT IN FINESSE FISHING.

This series incorporates cutting edge technology and the robust Ci4+ material, offering unmatched strength and lightness. Key innovations include the Duracross drag washer, Anti Twist Fin, Infinityxross, and Infinitydrive, enhancing performance and durability. The MGL rotor and Long Stroke Spool design promise smooth operation and superior casting. Tailored for both novices and seasoned anglers, the Vanford FA series sets new standards in the mid-range fishing reel market, ensuring every outing is both productive and enjoyable.

NOW FEATURING SIX MODELS, INCLUDING THE ULTRA LIGHT 500 SIZE.

500 | C2000HG | 2500HG | C3000HG | 4000 | C5000XG - RRP FROM $399.00

COMPLETE BOOK *of* FISHING KNOTS 2

First published in 2021 by
Australian Fishing Network
Reprint 2024

AFN Fishing & Outdoors
PO Box 544, Croydon, VIC 3136
Tel: +61 3 9729 8788
Email: sales@afn.com.au
www.afn.com.au

COMPLETE BOOK of
FISHING
KNOTS
Easy LEARN HOW! 2

Knots for
Freshwater & Saltwater

Everyone
Goes FISHING!

Nigel Webster & Bill Classon
Illustrated by Trevor Hawkins

AFN™
FISHING & OUTDOORS

CONTENTS

INTRODUCTION

Both Nigel and Bill hate losing fish! One of their most important hints is to tie quality fishing knots that won't let you down and the knots and the methods outlined in this book will increase your catch and decrease your break offs!

The biggest change in the last two decades in fishing has been the introduction of 'Super Lines' – a generic term for Braid and Gelspun and similar fishing lines, some regard the introduction of "Super Lines' as the biggest change since the introduction of graphite rods, with many saying it is even more important!

Braided multi-filament, non- stretch fishing lines have been with us for decades with Dacron braided products and the like. But it wasn't until Allied Signal/Johnson Worldwide/ Allied Signal released their Spectra based braid – Spiderwire at the US tackle Show in 1993 that we saw the high breaking strain for diameter product that has now almost taken over from monofilament as the world's most popular fishing line. The original Spiderwire was a classic 4 carrier braid that set the change in the way we fish forever! Their non-stretch properties magnify the bite and their breaking strain for diameter is unmatched in monofilament.

Now, there are hundreds of brands available, braided and fused from a variety of propriety products such as Spectra, Dyneema and other varieties of polypropylene. Our 'Super Lines' today are now made from a variety of processes –

1. True Braids – These can now be 4/5 and even 8 carrier (strands) and are braided using banks of braiding machines running around the clock.

2. Thermo-fused – A cost effective process that sees bunches of fibres passing through an element which heats, melts and fuses them together.

3. Coated Gel Spuns – Sees fibres moulded to a central fibre core, then aligned through a twist process.

Regardless of what variety of super line you use, one thing is non – negotiable – you will need to use a monofilament or fluorocarbon leader to effectively maximise your catch. Super lines are way more visible than mono or fluorocarbon.

The challenge is to join your 'Super Line' – Braid or Gelspun to that mono or fluoro leader effectively.

That is the MAIN reason for Nigel and Bill developing this Guide Book.

IMPORTANT TIPS FOR TYING YOUR KNOTS

LUBRICATION IS IMPORTANT

This is going back into basics 101. You need to ensure your knot is lubricated before you pull the knot tight. If you pull any knot while it is dry it will burn due to the friction and lose more than half its strength before you have even started. You can lubricate by applying some saliva and you can tell if you have burnt your knot as it loses its shape and goes wavy.

LOCK IT IN

After lubricating and tying your knot, make sure you safely wrap the line around your hands and pull as tight as you can to ensure the knot is locked and won't give way. If you need you can wear a glove and then wrap the line around your hand. This is the safest and best way to lock your knot off correctly.

VISUAL CHECK

It's always a good idea to examine your finished knot. Check it over and make sure it looks like it normally should. Check for incorrect loops, bunched knots, burnt or frayed lines. If you find something that isn't right, cut the knot and retie as it's not worth using a knot that isn't 100 per cent.

You may be thinking that's a lot of information and it's only about knots. The art of angling is a never ending journey though and there is endless things to learn to help you better your skills. To become a better angler you need to start at the bottom of the ladder with the basics and knots is the most important. If you're a native angler and want to feel confident using a good quality knot I highly recommend learning the bimini twist with fusion knot. It will be one of the most reliable knots you'll ever use!.

TOP SHOTTING

If you are fishing for light line species that won't run great distances (like bream) the general rule of thumb is to top shot with three cast lengths of braid (about 100 metres). The knot used to attach to the braid below can be the Double Uni knot on page 29. This is a good way of saving money or quickly changing line classes to better suit a fishing situation. This is commonly used by tournament anglers.

IMPROVING THE 'CASTABILITY' OF YOUR KNOT

Use surfboard wax to reduce rough edges of knots and improve casting efficiency and wear on knots.

STOPPING 'BRAID SLIPS' ON REELS

A metal spool with promote the whole spool of line slipping when braid is tied directly to spool. Many spools now have rubber strip around base to stop 'braid slip'. If you spool does not have this the way to fix is to run about 12-20 turns of monofilament line on the spool first and then connect to the braid using a Slim Beauty or Kanelt.

HOW COUNTER BRAID SHRINKAGE

Do not over-fill the reel spool. But initially you must fill it fully to allow for small amount of shrinkage as line tightens on to the spool after the first few uses.

GELSPUN LINE TO LEADER

GUIDE TO KNOTS

Gelspun to Single Strand Leader

KNOT	Strength	Bulk	Stress Resistance	Ease to tie	Notes
Double Uni	60%	Large	Good	Medium	Bulky – better option is KaneIt
Harro Knot	70%	Med/Large	Good	Medium/Hard	Anything Harro does is practical and quality.
Fusion Knot	60%	Med/Large	Good	Medium	A bulky but solid knot – not perfect for light lines.
Slim Beauty Full	75%	Small/Med	Excellent	Medium	A knot that won't let you down. Ideal for light to heavy line systems..
Slim Beauty Slim	65%	Small	Excellent	Medium	A knot that won't let you down. Ideal for light to heavy line systems. A small knot that hangs in there and is perfect for onto the spool length leaders with leaders under 12 kg.
Slim Beauty Double	80%	Med	Excellent	Medium	A knot that won't let you down and if tied with a double is ideal for subduing big fish. Bulletproof but bulks up with the double and if using leaders over 15 kg won't go through levelwind mechanisms but is fine through rodguides.
Slim Beauty Easy	60%	Small	Excellent	Easy	A knot that won't let you down. Ideal for light to heavy line systems. A small knot that hangs in there and is perfect for onto the spool length leaders with leaders under 12 kg.
KaneIt	70%	Small	Excellent	Medium	A knot that won't let you down. Ideal for light to heavy line systems. A small knot that hangs in there and is perfect for onto the spool length leaders with leaders under 12 kg.
KaneItEasy	65%	Small	Excellent	Easy	A knot that won't let you down. Ideal for light to heavy line systems. A small knot that hangs in there and is perfect for onto the spool length leaders with leaders under 12 kg.
FG	100%	Small	Excellent	Hard	Ideal for med/heavy leaders to braid.
FG Easy	95%	Small	Excellent	Medium	Ideal for med/heavy leaders to braid.
Wind-on leaders	100%	Small	Ultimate	Medium	A considered system, perfect in every respect but not suitable for leaders under 8–10 kg breaking strain. Also note that this is not a leader that can be quickly changed on the day, but extremely long lasting and virtually bulletproof.
Albright knot	55%	Medium	Poor	Medium	If used for repeated casting will let go.
Albright Reverse	55%	Medium	Medium	Medium	Much more durable than Albright.
Mike Connolly's knot	55%	Large	Reasonable	Complex	Bulky knot
Ted Donelan knot	50-90%	Medium	Medium	Medium	Requires a double to be tied in gelspun and found it prone to slipping with many of the new braids and gelspuns. Variation is due to slippage on some gelspuns.

NOTE: *Most knots here are designated 100% of the manufacturer's rated breaking strain as the double in the gelspun effectively doubles the breaking strain of the system—so a KaneIt Knot @ 65% will test on the system over 100% of a single strand (50% will the manufacturer's rated breaking strain).*

DOUBLE UNI KNOT

This is a relatively easy knot to tie and is used for joining lines of similar or different diameters. It holds very well and is best used for lighter lines up to 12–15 kilograms breaking strain. It cast through the rod guides very nicely which makes for greater accuracy. When trimming the tags on this knot, cut them closely but leave a small tag to prevent the knot slipping. This knot is sometimes known as a Grinner Knot.

PERFORMANCE
A solid and useful knot but somewhat on the bulky side due to the full 5–6 wraps on the mono leader side of the knot. Suggest Kanelt is a better option.
The efficiency of this knot decreases as the diameter of the mono leader increases and the diameter of braid to leader becomes disproportionate.

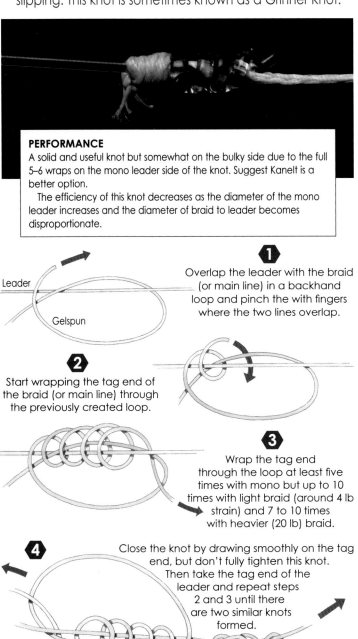

① Overlap the leader with the braid (or main line) in a backhand loop and pinch the with fingers where the two lines overlap.

② Start wrapping the tag end of the braid (or main line) through the previously created loop.

③ Wrap the tag end through the loop at least five times with mono but up to 10 times with light braid (around 4 lb strain) and 7 to 10 times with heavier (20 lb) braid.

④ Close the knot by drawing smoothly on the tag end, but don't fully tighten this knot. Then take the tag end of the leader and repeat steps 2 and 3 until there are two similar knots formed.

⑤ Close the second knot slightly. Take the two tag ends of the knots and pull away from each other so that the two knots close and tighten on the line and slide up to each other. Make sure both knots tighten neatly against the line and each other.

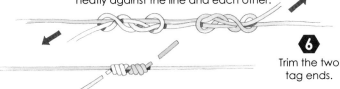

⑥ Trim the two tag ends.

HARRO KNOT

An effective knot for joining a single strand gelspun line to a heavy mono leader.

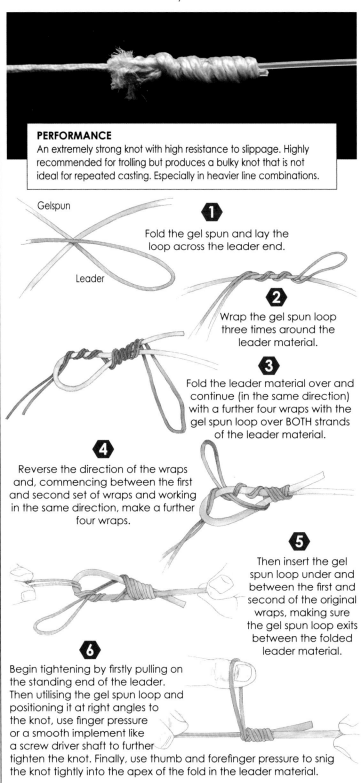

PERFORMANCE
An extremely strong knot with high resistance to slippage. Highly recommended for trolling but produces a bulky knot that is not ideal for repeated casting. Especially in heavier line combinations.

① Fold the gel spun and lay the loop across the leader end.

② Wrap the gel spun loop three times around the leader material.

③ Fold the leader material over and continue (in the same direction) with a further four wraps with the gel spun loop over BOTH strands of the leader material.

④ Reverse the direction of the wraps and, commencing between the first and second set of wraps and working in the same direction, make a further four wraps.

⑤ Then insert the gel spun loop under and between the first and second of the original wraps, making sure the gel spun loop exits between the folded leader material.

⑥ Begin tightening by firstly pulling on the standing end of the leader. Then utilising the gel spun loop and positioning it at right angles to the knot, use finger pressure or a smooth implement like a screw driver shaft to further tighten the knot. Finally, use thumb and forefinger pressure to snig the knot tightly into the apex of the fold in the leader material.

⑦ Bend the standing end of the leader material to facilitate the removal of the mono tag flush with the end of the gel spun wraps. Leave tag ends of a couple of millimetres in the gel spun. This is insurance against unravelling. Gel spuns do not always seat with the certainty and permanence of monofilaments. Every which way, this is the superior gel spun/heavy mono leader connection.

FUSION KNOT

This knot was developed by Rhys Creed and unlike the FG Knot and Albright Knot that have the braid wrapped around the outside of the knot and around the leader, the Fusion Knot has the leader wrapping around the braid which creates a very abrasion resistant knot that will handle rough treatment on structure.

Matched with a Bimini Twist this is an extremely tough knot when using 30 lb braid to 40 lb leaders.

PERFORMANCE
The Fusion exhibits a similar construction to the Harro Knot. Again it needs to be tied with the gelspun simply doubled over as Rhys specifies with a full double formed via a Bimini Twist. It is a strong knot that exhibits good hold with larger diameters and leader sizes.

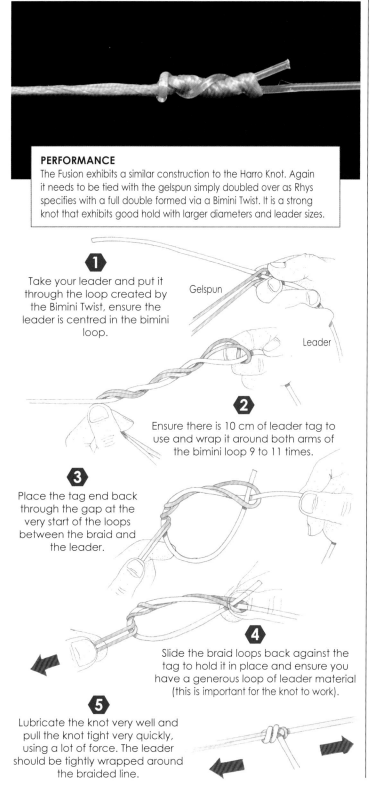

① Take your leader and put it through the loop created by the Bimini Twist, ensure the leader is centred in the bimini loop.

Gelspun

Leader

② Ensure there is 10 cm of leader tag to use and wrap it around both arms of the bimini loop 9 to 11 times.

③ Place the tag end back through the gap at the very start of the loops between the braid and the leader.

④ Slide the braid loops back against the tag to hold it in place and ensure you have a generous loop of leader material (this is important for the knot to work).

⑤ Lubricate the knot very well and pull the knot tight very quickly, using a lot of force. The leader should be tightly wrapped around the braided line.

SLIM BEAUTY
Full Version

The Slim Beauty is an easy knot to tie that offers good strength, and casts well in most situations. It becomes difficult to tie, only in very fine diameters where it is difficult to thread the braid through the Figure of Eight. This knot is ideal for most lure and bait fishing applications. It becomes an issue for anglers who are casting when leader knots are created using heavy line classes which become bulky; this tends to occur when tying a leader knot on line classes of 50 pounds and larger. In the event that we plan to troll, jig or bait fish when using heavier leaders, rather than high speed casting, then the Slim Beauty is a great option despite the larger knot size.

NIGEL WEBSTER RECOMMENDED KNOT ★★

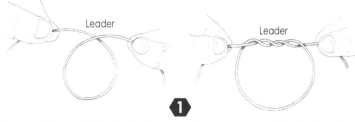

PERFORMANCE
Highly recommended for light line performance. It is a very strong knot that if tied correctly won't slip and a knot that does not weaken with repeated casting. It does become a little bulky in heavy combinations (30 pound braid and 40/50 pound leaders).

Leader   Leader

① Form a Figure of Eight in the leader is the common start to both knots. Form a loop and a double overhand or granny knot.

② Pull the knot up carefully.

③ Until finally, an 'eight' forms— leave the two openings with enough room to pass the gelspun through.

Gelspun

Leader

④ Then pass the gelspun up through the second opening.

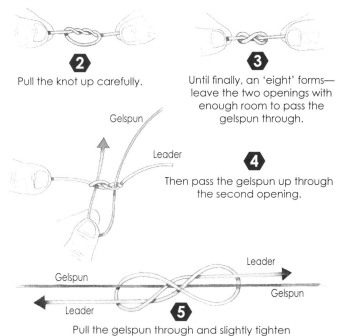

Leader

Gelspun

Gelspun

Leader

⑤ Pull the gelspun through and slightly tighten the eight.

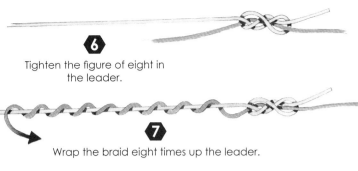

6 Tighten the figure of eight in the leader.

7 Wrap the braid eight times up the leader.

8 Then wrap the braid back down to the eight 5–6 times.

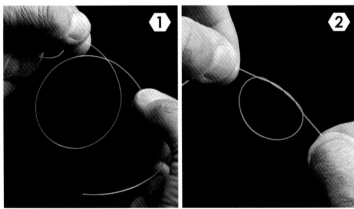

9 Pull the knot up carefully and trim.

Forming a figure-of-eight in the leader is the common start to both knots. Form a loop and a double overhand or granny knot.

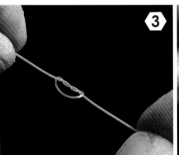

Pull the knot up carefully.

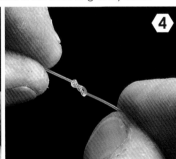

Until finally an 'eight' forms – leave the two openings ...

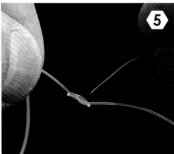

... with enough room to pass the gelspun through.

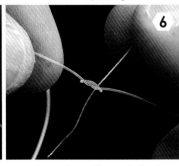

Pass the gelspun through the tag end opening of the eight.

Then pass the gelspun up through the second opening.

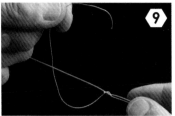

Pull the gelspun through and slightly tighten the eight.

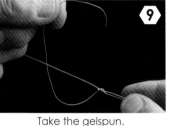

Take the gelspun.

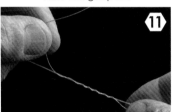

Wind it up the leader.

At least ten times.

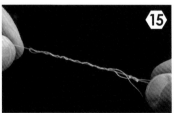

Then hold the leader and gelspun and wind the gelspun back ...

... down 5–6 times ...

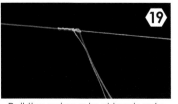

... to the eight.

Pass through the first loop.

Tighten the eight and pull up on the leader and the gelspun.

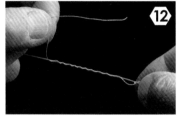

Lightly pull on the gelspun tag to ensure an orderly and neat configuration.

Continue pulling up on the leader and the gelspun main line.

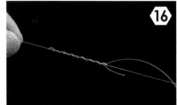

Pull the gelspun knot back onto the eight.

Finally, pull up really tight and trim.

SLIM BEAUTY
Slim Version

This version eliminates the wraps that takes the gelspun back down to the figure of eight 'locker'. This produces a less bulky knot.

NIGEL WEBSTER RECOMMENDED KNOT ★ ★ ★

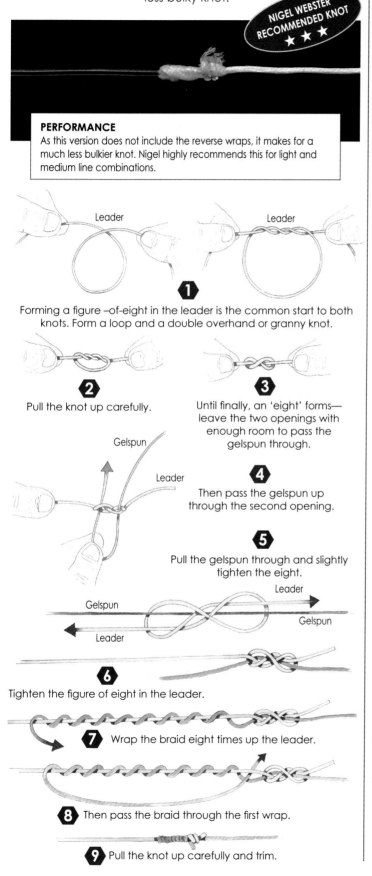

PERFORMANCE
As this version does not include the reverse wraps, it makes for a much less bulkier knot. Nigel highly recommends this for light and medium line combinations.

1 Forming a figure –of-eight in the leader is the common start to both knots. Form a loop and a double overhand or granny knot.

2 Pull the knot up carefully.

3 Until finally, an 'eight' forms—leave the two openings with enough room to pass the gelspun through.

4 Then pass the gelspun up through the second opening.

5 Pull the gelspun through and slightly tighten the eight.

6 Tighten the figure of eight in the leader.

7 Wrap the braid eight times up the leader.

8 Then pass the braid through the first wrap.

9 Pull the knot up carefully and trim.

SLIM BEAUTY
Double Version

For added strength, you can double the braid, but it will make the knot bulkier. Mainly suitable for trolling.

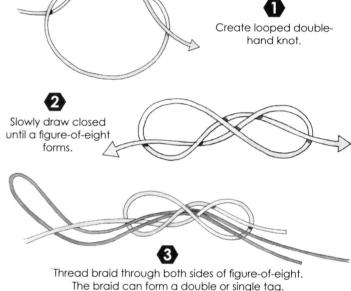

1 Create looped double-hand knot.

2 Slowly draw closed until a figure-of-eight forms.

3 Thread braid through both sides of figure-of-eight. The braid can form a double or single tag. Note this diagram showcases a braided double.

4 Wrap along monofilament seven times while leaving a gap between figure-of-eight and leader material. Reverse wrap and begin cross-wrapping previous section.

5 Return wrap back to figure-of-eight by cross-wrapping five times. Thread braid tag end through the gap left between braid and leader.

6 Slowly draw figure-of-eight closed. Lubricate braid and slowly draw braid tight against closed figure-of-eight. Slowly but firmly tighten by pulling both ends of line. Clip tag ends.

SLIM BEAUTY
Easy Version

This knot for joining braids and mono leaders is a quick and far easier alternative to standard Slim Beauty knots where you are fishing in low light situations, have poorer eyesight, are on a rocking boat, in the wind, or when using light lines around 1 to 4 kilograms where threading the figure eight in the mono becomes problematic for even the best knot tiers. This 'easy' Slim Beauty eliminates that threading of the figure eight totally.

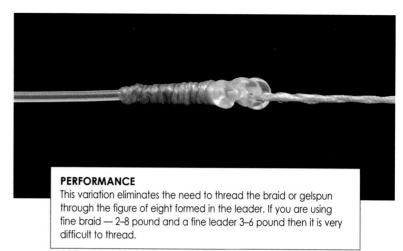

PERFORMANCE
This variation eliminates the need to thread the braid or gelspun through the figure of eight formed in the leader. If you are using fine braid — 2–8 pound and a fine leader 3–6 pound then it is very difficult to thread.

Leader

Gelspun

1 Lay the leader alongside the gelspun.

2 Form a loop with the leader alongside the braid.

3 Then perform a simple double Granny Knot around the gelspun.

Gelspun

Leader

Gelspun

Leader

4 Pull up both ends of the leader.

5 So that the figure of eight in the leader tightens on the gelspun.

6 Wrap the braid eight times up the leader.

7 Then wrap the braid back down to the eight 5–6 times.

8 Pull the knot up carefully and trim.

HANDY HINT
For performance casting when using complex knots, try running the knot through a block of surfers board wax to form a slippery coating to enhance its passage through the rod guides.

KANEIT KNOT
Single strand gelspun to leader (after common start)

This knot was developed by Darwin angler, Kane Dysart, for all forms of tackle and species. The knot is essentially a 'slimmed down' version of a Uni Knot.
It has exceptional strength and resilience. It has a smaller profile than many, including the Slim Beauty.

PERFORMANCE

When tied in low breaking strain combinations 2–10 pound braid and 4–20 pound leaders the small profile of the knot allows for longer leaders as the knot can be safely cast off the spool.

The Figure 8 lock profile of this knot means that it doesn't get damaged by repeated casts (as the Albright suffers from).

In heavier combinations the knot however, needs to sit off the spool of your threadline or baitcaster as it is too bulky to cast directly off the spool.

1

Forming a figure –of-eight in the leader is the common start to both knots. Form a loop and a double overhand or granny knot.

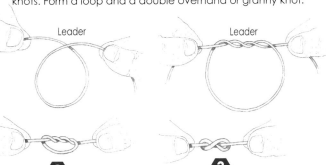

Leader   Leader

2

Pull the knot up carefully.

3

Until finally, an 'eight' forms— leave the two openings ...

4

... with enough room to pass the gelspun through.

Pass the gelspun through the tag end opening of the eight.

Gelspun

Leader

5

Then pass the gelspun up through the second opening.

6

Take the gelspun ...

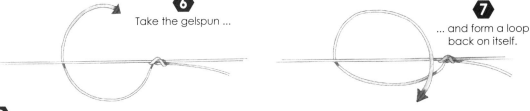

7

... and form a loop back on itself.

8

Then wind the gelspun up on itself and the leader ten times.

9

Take the gelspun tag and pull up…

10

... forming a knot on the leader.

11

Continue to pull up…

12

... until the knot forms.

13

Take the gelspun main line and the leader…

... and pull up each so that the two knots…

14

... lock up on one another. Trim the knots and go fishing.

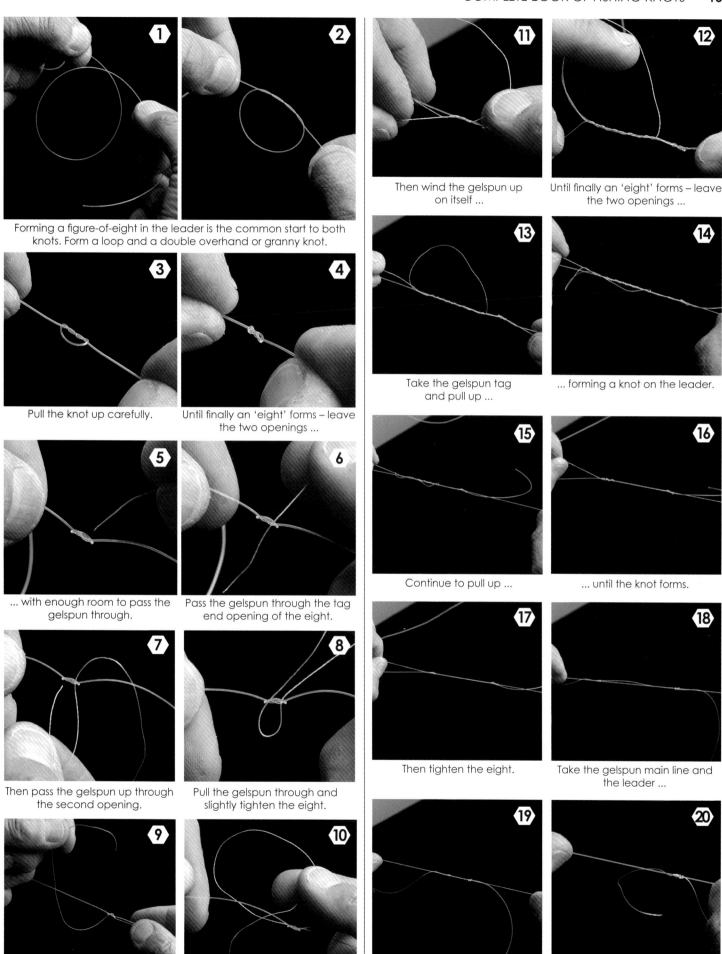

1

Forming a figure-of-eight in the leader is the common start to both knots. Form a loop and a double overhand or granny knot.

3 Pull the knot up carefully.

4 Until finally an 'eight' forms – leave the two openings ...

5 ... with enough room to pass the gelspun through.

6 Pass the gelspun through the tag end opening of the eight.

7 Then pass the gelspun up through the second opening.

8 Pull the gelspun through and slightly tighten the eight.

9 Take the gelspun ...

10 ... and form a loop back on itself.

11 Then wind the gelspun up on itself ...

12 Until finally an 'eight' forms – leave the two openings ...

13 Take the gelspun tag and pull up ...

14 ... forming a knot on the leader.

15 Continue to pull up ...

16 ... until the knot forms.

17 Then tighten the eight.

18 Take the gelspun main line and the leader ...

19 ... and pull up each so that the two knots ...

20 ... lock up on one another. Trim the knot and go fishing.

EASY KANEIT KNOT

In lighter combinations it can be quite difficult to thread the braid through the tiny figure of eight if the leader is in the 4–8 pound range. So simply form the Figure of Eight by wrapping a double overhand granny knot over the gelspun.

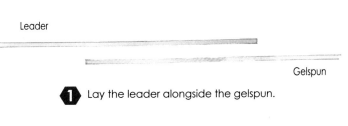

1 Lay the leader alongside the gelspun.

PERFORMANCE
Bill Classon uses this variation for all his light line combinations from bream to flathead and trout to golden perch.

It is not quite as good as forming the Figure of Eight and threading the gelspun through. But it is very close!

It holds up tremendously well under repeated casts. Its super slim profile allows for long leaders as it can be safely and confidently cast off a threadline or baitcaster.

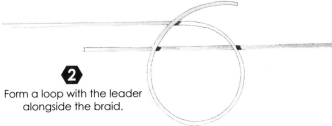

2 Form a loop with the leader alongside the braid.

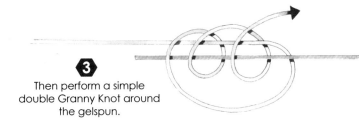

3 Then perform a simple double Granny Knot around the gelspun.

4 Pull up both ends of the leader.

5 So that the figure of eight in the leader tightens on the gelspun.

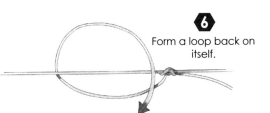

6 Form a loop back on itself.

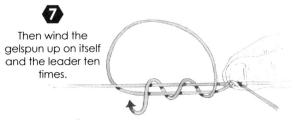

7 Then wind the gelspun up on itself and the leader ten times.

8 Take the gelspun tag and pull up…

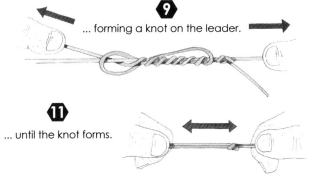

9 … forming a knot on the leader.

10 Continue to pull up…

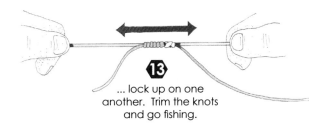

11 … until the knot forms.

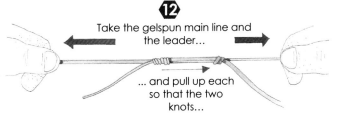

12 Take the gelspun main line and the leader… … and pull up each so that the two knots…

13 … lock up on one another. Trim the knots and go fishing.

FG KNOT

This is an ideal knot for attaching heavy leaders of 15 kg breaking strain braid and greater. It is a great knot for heavy sportfishing applications. It is a hard knot to master but one that exhibits top performance.

NIGEL WEBSTER RECOMMENDED KNOT ★★★

PERFORMANCE

The FG is a braid to monofilament/fluorocarbon leader connection knot. It is a tension knot: designed to hold two separate lines together through pure line wrap and tension. This means that the FG is exceptionally thin and strong which has great applications for fishing techniques that require excessive casting with all line classes.

It is particularly effective when using heavy line classes during fishing applications such as lure casting for large fish such as giant trevally, mackerel and the like. Alternatively, many anglers using baitcast style fishing reels for fresh and saltwater species are now choosing to use FG knots when fishing.

The advantage of this knot includes the option to select longer leader lengths. The slim-line leader knot does not cause friction burn to the thumb when running this knot across fingers during casting with a baitcast reel. This means that the angler can retrieve the knot on to the spool of the reel and thereby use longer leader lengths should that be desired.

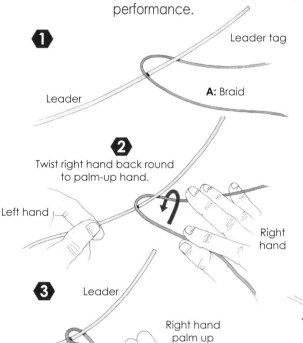

1

Leader tag

Leader

A: Braid

2 Twist right hand back round to palm-up hand.

Left hand

Right hand

3

Leader

Right hand palm up

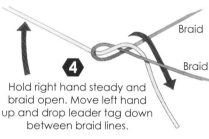

4 Hold right hand steady and braid open. Move left hand up and drop leader tag down between braid lines.

Braid

Braid

5 Twist right hand palm-up 180 degrees to back hand-up.

Leader

6 Right hand twist in Step 5 will capture tag. Hold right hand steady and braid open, move left hand down and push leader tag up between braid lines.

Leader

Braid

Leader

7 Continue process of right hand twisting leader tag down, right hand twist leader tag up until 6 right hand twists are in place.

Leader

Braid

8 Hold both braid main line and braid tag tight in right hand. Pull looping section up and down leader while gradually tightening – this will prevent bunching. Pull tight until looping section locks in place on leader.

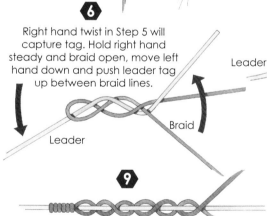

9

Repeat steps 3 to 8 again, creating another 6 twist looped section and ensure locks into place above first 6 twist section. Repeat the process once more and add another 6 twists so that the closed wraps include 18 twists.

10

Leader tag

A: Braid mainline

B: Braid tag

Steps 10 to 11: Repeat cross reverse half-hitches 6 to 8 times

11

Leader tag

A: Braid mainline

B: Braid tag

Steps 12 to 14: Half-hitch the braided mainline 6 times, draw entire knot tight and clip tag ends.

12 Half hitches

B: Braid tag

A: Braid mainline

13

B: Braid tag

A: Braid mainline

14

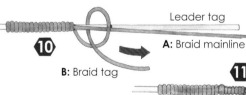

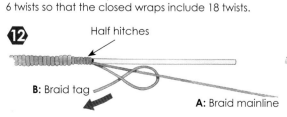

A: Braid mainline

EASY FG KNOT

BILL CLASSON HIGHLY RECOMMENDED ★ ★ ★

This method of tying is a far easier way to tie high performance sportfishing knot.

Simply arrange things so that one side of the braid is locked to your reel and rod in a rod holder or if at home simply fix in place behind a heavy object like a couch.

Pull about 5 metres of braid off the reel and then tie it to another immovable object.

Then simply lay the leader at right angles to the braid and start forming the plait by passing the leader over and under the braid.

PERFORMANCE

This is a true high performance sportfishing leader knot. Due to its slim profile it can be wound on to threadlines and baitcasters in light and medium combinations (10–50 pound braid combined with 30–60 pound leader).

Over that it is best not to have a leader length that allows the knot to position on your spool. With heavy popping outfits and hard casting it is recommended to keep the knot off the spool.

The great attributes this knot delivers is immense strength and reliability, it does not catch on rod guides, it has the slimmest profile of any leader knot and hardly deteriorates even with repeated casts.

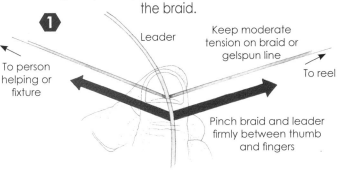

1 Leader

Keep moderate tension on braid or gelspun line

To person helping or fixture

To reel

Pinch braid and leader firmly between thumb and fingers

3 Pull each twist down firmly and lock between thumb and fingers as you progress with turns

120°

4 This illustration shows twists loose to show what's happening

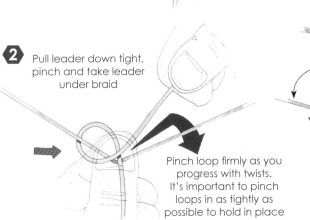

2 Pull leader down tight, pinch and take leader under braid

Pinch loop firmly as you progress with twists. It's important to pinch loops in as tightly as possible to hold in place

5 This illustration shows twists working up line without tension. When tying knot these loose loops would not be forming. They would all be tight between thumb and fingers.

Pull tight and pinch every twist as you progress with braids. As you progress the formed twists will work out to the rear of your thumb and forefinger

Progress in the same fashion for 20-50 turns depending on line breaking strain. You must continue to firmly pinch each twist between your thumb and fingers as you progress

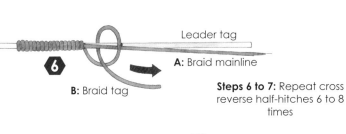

6 Leader tag

A: Braid mainline

B: Braid tag

Steps 6 to 7: Repeat cross reverse half-hitches 6 to 8 times

7 Leader tag

A: Braid mainline

B: Braid tag

Steps 8 to 10: Half-hitch the braided mainline 6 times, draw entire knot tight and clip tag ends.

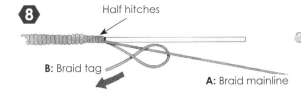

8 Half hitches

B: Braid tag

A: Braid mainline

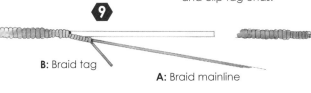

9 B: Braid tag

A: Braid mainline

10 A: Braid mainline

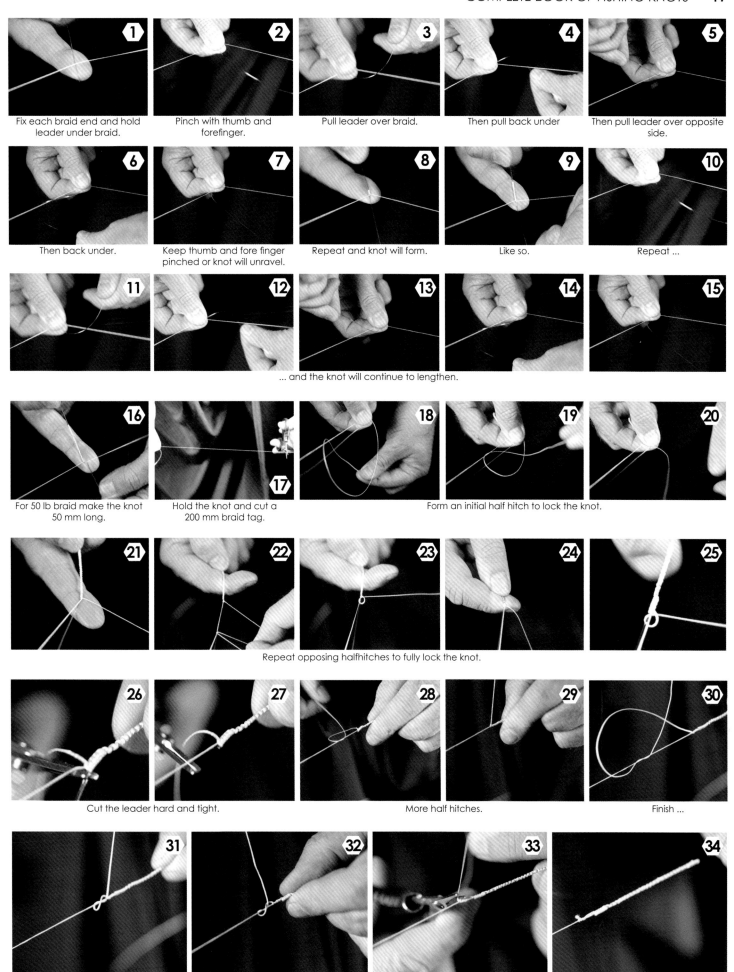

1 Fix each braid end and hold leader under braid.

2 Pinch with thumb and forefinger.

3 Pull leader over braid.

4 Then pull back under

5 Then pull leader over opposite side.

6 Then back under.

7 Keep thumb and fore finger pinched or knot will unravel.

8 Repeat and knot will form.

9 Like so.

10 Repeat ...

11 **12** **13** **14** **15**

... and the knot will continue to lengthen.

16 For 50 lb braid make the knot 50 mm long.

17 Hold the knot and cut a 200 mm braid tag.

18 **19** **20** Form an initial half hitch to lock the knot.

21 **22** **23** **24** **25**

Repeat opposing halfhitches to fully lock the knot.

26 Cut the leader hard and tight.

27 **28** More half hitches.

29 **30** Finish ...

31 **32** **33** **34**

... with opposing double half hitches.

THE BD KNOT

Everyone needs a good knot to join braid to leader. The FG is the best – But this BD Knot is a lot simpler and easier to tie and most importantly it's faster!

Developed by tackle technician Mick Caulfield it's ideal for light and medium line applications.

It also ticks a lot of boxes.

Firstly it's fast, simple and easy to tie!

Secondly it doesn't deteriorate over time. In other words the configuration of the knot doesn't allow it to affected to damage by repeated casts and the knot passing through the rod guides repeatedly.

Lastly, it's super strong!

PERFORMANCE

This knot also exhibits a very high percentage knot strength and it is suitable for both light and medium leaders diameters. When pulled tight it won't slip.

Most importantly it is a small profile footprint that keep bulk to a minimum and hence makes it easy to cast off the spool and through rod guides.

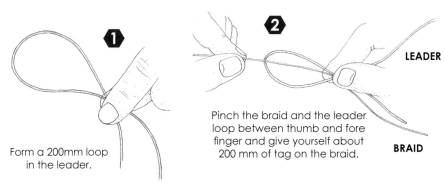

Form a 200mm loop in the leader.

Pinch the braid and the leader loop between thumb and fore finger and give yourself about 200 mm of tag on the braid.

LEADER

BRAID

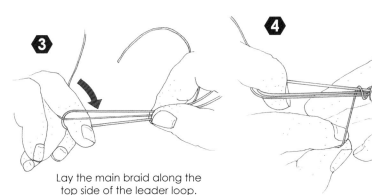

Lay the main braid along the top side of the leader loop.

Hold the leader loop in the crux of the main finger of second hand.

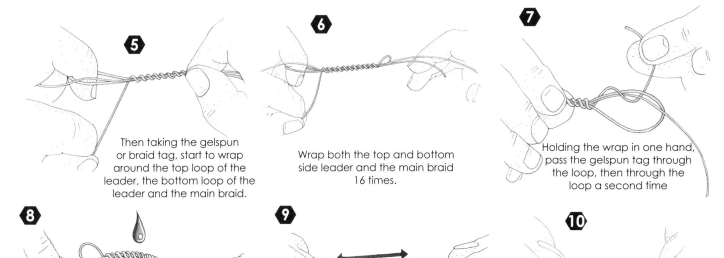

Then taking the gelspun or braid tag, start to wrap around the top loop of the leader, the bottom loop of the leader and the main braid.

Wrap both the top and bottom side leader and the main braid 16 times.

Holding the wrap in one hand, pass the gelspun tag through the loop, then through the loop a second time

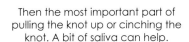

Then the most important part of pulling the knot up or cinching the knot. A bit of saliva can help.

You need to cynch the knot slowly and carefully as the knot tightens from the inside. It is important to hold both the gelspun and leader and their tags in each hand to pull up neatly and cleanly.

The completed knot. The loop can now be adjusted for length by simply pulling the tag with a pair of pliers. Then re tighten knot.

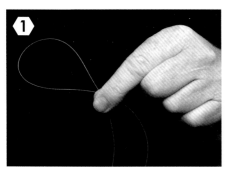

Form a 200mm loop in the leader.

Pinch the braid and the leader loop between thumb and fore finger and give yourself about 200 mm of tag on the braid.

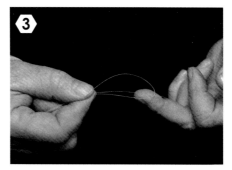

Lay the main braid along the top side of the leader loop.

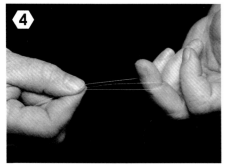

Hold the leader loop in the crux of the main finger of second hand.

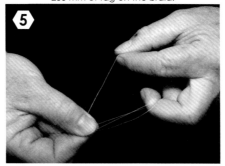

Also hold the main braid along the top side of the leader loop.

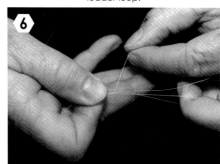

Then taking the gelspun or braid tag, start to wrap around the top loop of the leader, the bottom loop of the leader and the main braid.

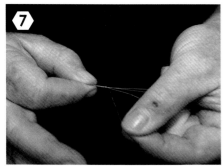

Then taking the gelspun or braid tag, start to wrap around the top loop of the leader, the bottom loop of the leader and the main braid.

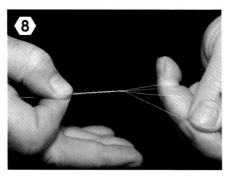

Wrap both the top and bottom side leader and the main braid 16 times.

Holding the wrap in one hand, pass the gelspun tag through the loop, then through the loop a second time

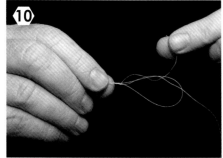

then through the loop a second time

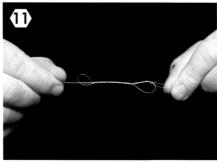

Then the most important part of pulling the knot up or cinching the knot

Releasing the loops but still holding teh leader begin to pull up on the knot

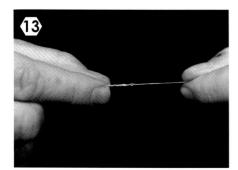

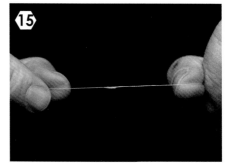

You need to cynch the knot slowly and carefully as the knot tightens from the inside. It is important to hold both the gelspun and leader and their tags in each hand to pull up neatly and cleanly.

Finally when the knot has been tighened and fully formed, lock it by just pulling on the leader and main gelspun only.

QUICK FG KNOT

This method of tying the FG Knot was developed by Mick Caulfield. It is an ideal solution for those who want to tie the knot "On – the – Run" whether that be in the boat or on a jetty

They key to tying an effective FG is to secure both ends of the braid, with this Mick simply places the reel that holds the braid on a rod and secure in a rod holder. The other end is tied to a Bulldog clip which can be secured to your shirt collar.

PERFORMANCE

This is a true high-performance sportfishing knot. It has a slim profile, and the knot can be wound onto threadlines and baitcasters in light and light-medium combinations.

Over that it is best to use a leader length that will position the knot away from the spool. For example, with heavy popping outfits and hard casting it is recommended to keep the knot off the spool.

The FG exhibits immense strength and reliability and hardly deteriorates over time.

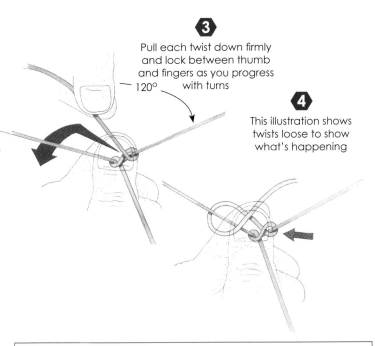

3 Pull each twist down firmly and lock between thumb and fingers as you progress with turns
120°

4 This illustration shows twists loose to show what's happening

---

PERFORMANCE

This is a true high performance sportfishing leader knot. Due to its slim profile it can be wound on to threadlines and baitcasters in light and medium combinations (10–50 pound braid combined with 30–60 pound leader).

Over that it is best not to have a leader length that allows the knot to position off your spool. For example with heavy popping outfits and hard casting it is recommended to keep the knot off the spool.

The great attributes this knot delivers is immense strength and reliability, it does not catch on rod guides, it has the slimmest profile of any leader knot and hardly deteriorates even with repeated casts.

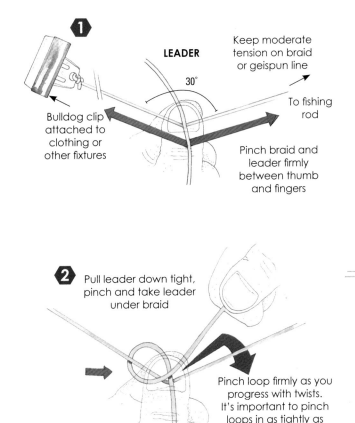

1

Bulldog clip attached to clothing or other fixtures

LEADER

30°

Keep moderate tension on braid or geispun line

To fishing rod

Pinch braid and leader firmly between thumb and fingers

2 Pull leader down tight, pinch and take leader under braid

Pinch loop firmly as you progress with twists. It's important to pinch loops in as tightly as possible to hold in place

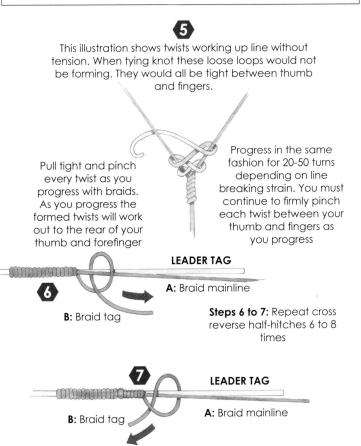

5 This illustration shows twists working up line without tension. When tying knot these loose loops would not be forming. They would all be tight between thumb and fingers.

Pull tight and pinch every twist as you progress with braids. As you progress the formed twists will work out to the rear of your thumb and forefinger

Progress in the same fashion for 20-50 turns depending on line breaking strain. You must continue to firmly pinch each twist between your thumb and fingers as you progress

6

LEADER TAG

A: Braid mainline

B: Braid tag

Steps 6 to 7: Repeat cross reverse half-hitches 6 to 8 times

7

LEADER TAG

A: Braid mainline

B: Braid tag

8 Half hitches — Cut leader tag then half hitch to finish

B: Braid tag

A: Braid mainline

Steps 8 to 10: Half-hitch the braided mainline 6 times, draw entire knot tight and clip tag ends.

9

B: Braid tag

A: Braid mainline

10

A: Braid mainline

1 Pass the braid through the eye of the clip

2 Then tie a uni knot to secure the braid to the clip

3 Clamp the clip to your collar of your shirt, and secure your road in a rod holder with a locked drag

Then grab your leader and clamp the spool firmly between your legs

4

5 Form a V in the braid and loop the leader over the braid

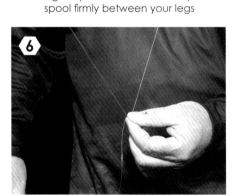

6 Grasp the three pieces at the V with your left hand

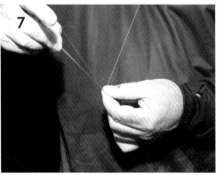

7 Start passing the leader over and under and back over each side of the braid

8 Do this by tighly pulling the elader through the middle and back under the right side

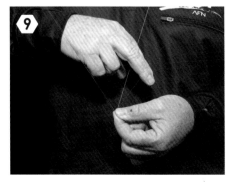

9 Around and under

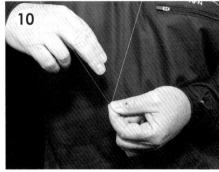

10 Back to the middle then through again

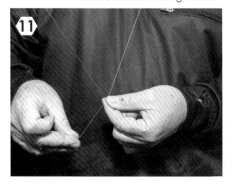

11 Then back under the left side

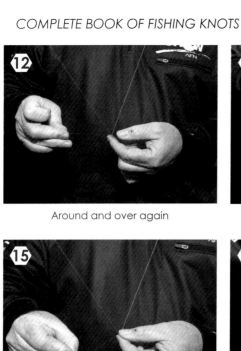

Around and over again

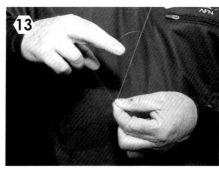

and through again

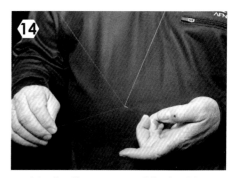

Monitor the progress of the knot by holding both ends of leader

Then proceed to build the knot

The trick to this knot is remember just pass the leader tag through the middle of the V

Under the braid

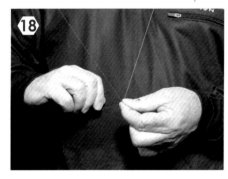

over

Through the middle

After at least 10-12 turns each side

20 turns in total

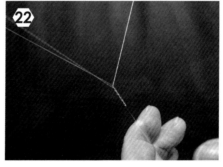

Once this is completed

Cinch the knot down by pulling the leader firmly down on the FG knot

Release the tag end of the braid

Then align the tag of the leader along the main part of the braid

Holding leader tag and main braid from a half-hitch with the braid tag

Cinch and pull up. Cinch hard on the first half hitch

To remove all the stretch in the knot

The knot is now secured, and from a 2nd half hitch in to the opposite

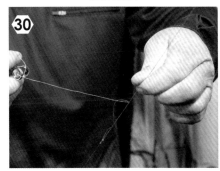

Form another half hitch 4 alternating half hitches

Pull down and trim the leader tag off neat to the top of the knot

Then form another 4 alternate half hitches

On each side of the braid

The form a double half hitch on one side

Pull up

Form a double half hitch the other side

and pull up tight to fisnihg the knot

Trim the braid tag leaving 4mm protruding

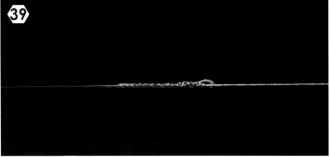

The completed FG knot. The reason for the 4mm tag is that you can monitor state of the knot while fishing

WIND ON LEADER KNOT

BILL CLASSON
RECOMMENDED
★ ★ ★

Criss-Cross Braid Join

The best system bar none for attaching a braid bind (Criss Cross loop). The best doubles for this system are a Plait or a Bimini Twist.

Wind-on leader systems are smooth, seamless, guaranteed 100% and have amazing longevity (over 1000 casts) and relatively easy to join once you have formed the double. The only downfall of wind-on leaders at present, is that they cannot be purchased below 10 kg breaking strain.

PERFORMANCE

Another high end method of joining braid to heavy leader. This system does of course require the braid to have a double formed first either by a Bimini Twist or by Plaiting. It also requires the angler to purchase quality wind on leaders.

This system is most commonly used in game fishing siuations where the length of the dacron loop on the leader is irrelevant. In a sportfishing situation however, the dacron loop should not exceed 50–60 mm otherwise the system is too bulky.

Wind on leader systems are not condusive for casting situations, but are the ultimate connection for medium/heavy jigging, trolling and gamefishing situations.

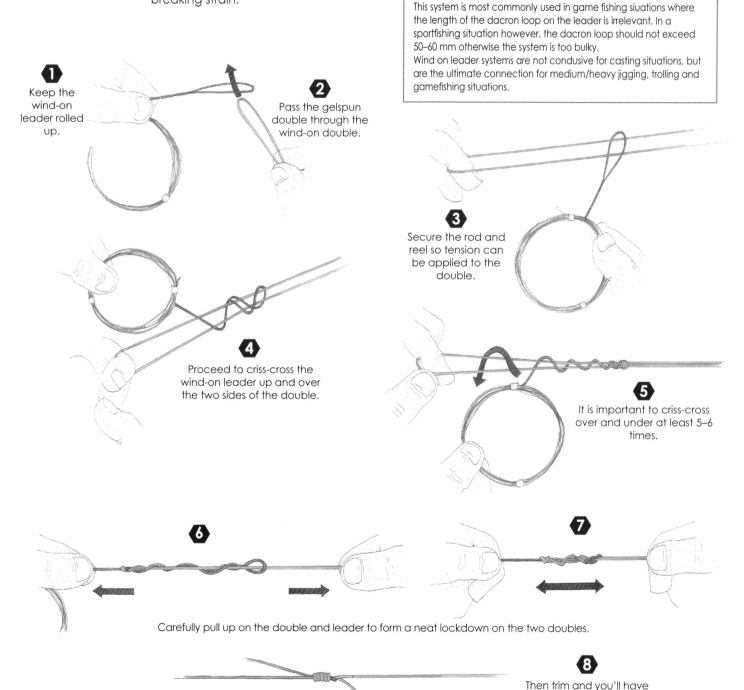

1 Keep the wind-on leader rolled up.

2 Pass the gelspun double through the wind-on double.

3 Secure the rod and reel so tension can be applied to the double.

4 Proceed to criss-cross the wind-on leader up and over the two sides of the double.

5 It is important to criss-cross over and under at least 5–6 times.

6 **7** Carefully pull up on the double and leader to form a neat lockdown on the two doubles.

8 Then trim and you'll have a 100 per cent, 1000 cast system!

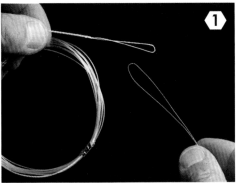

Keep the wind-on leader rolled up.

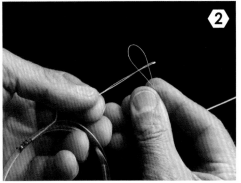

Pass the gelspun double through the wind-on double.

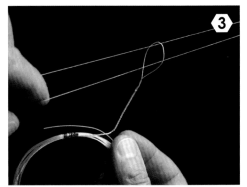

Secure the rod and reel so tension can be applied to the double.

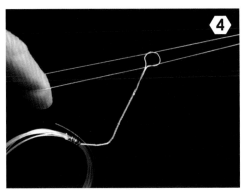

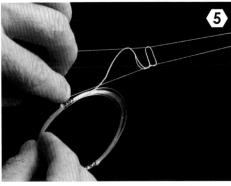

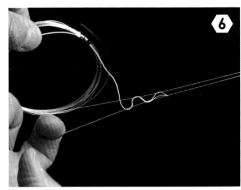

Proceed to criss-cross the wind-on leader up and over the two sides of the double.

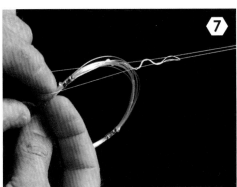

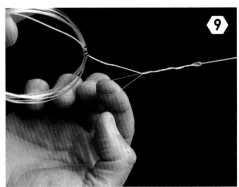

It is important to criss-cross over and under at least 5–6 times.

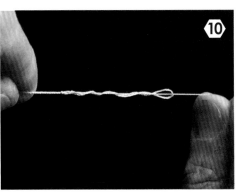

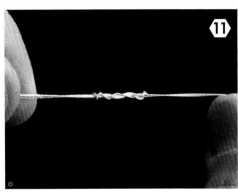

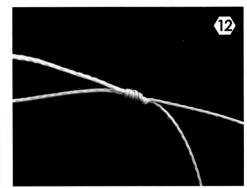

Carefully pull up on the double and leader to form a neat lockdown on the two doubles.
Then trim and you'll have a 100 per cent, 1000 cast system!

HANDY HINT

LENGTH OF LEADER

When it comes to choosing the length of your leader, the rule of thumb is to use a rod length. The reason for this is simple: you don't want to run the leader knot that you have tied onto your reel. This will cause it to wear faster and cause it to catch on your guide when you cast, especially with heavier lines. Not only does it affect your cast and your knot, it can also cause damage to the worm drive on your reel. Measure the leader knot right to the edge of the reel and give yourself an extra 10 cm as you will use this extra line to tie your lure on with.

REVERSE ALBRIGHT KNOT

This knot is a variation on the traditional Albright Knot as shown elsewhere in this book.

A standard Albright Knot is not recommended for joining braid and leaders as its configuration causes the knot to break down with repeated casts. Far better to use the Reverse Albright.

This version sees the braid taken up the leader and then wound back down to the leader loop.

It is also possible to tie this knot with the main line (braid or mono doubled).

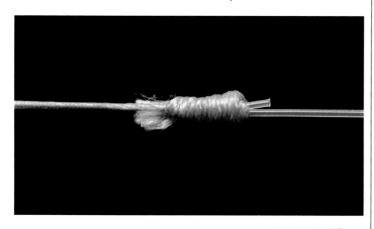

①

Take the mono leader and the braid and place them together as shown. Making sure you have enough line to complete the knot.

②

Double the mono leader back on itself at the knot end and pinch the tag end of the mono and the main leader length and the braid and start the wraps.

③

Keep wrapping the braid back towards main line as shown and continue to perform roughly 20 wraps ensuring that each is after the last and not overlapping.

After you've done 20 wraps take the tag (or tag ends through if mainline has been doubled) through the original leader loop as shown and start to draw the knot closed by holding the double leader ends and pulling on the tag(s) of the main line.

④

Draw the knot up as tight as possible and test a few times to make sure it's locked firmly. Trim the tags leaving about 2mm hanging.

MIKE CONNOLLY'S LEADER KNOT

A relatively easy knot to tie that forms a slim profile. It's one downside is that both tags face forward, towards the rod tip, and as such tend to 'knock' on the rod guides when casting.

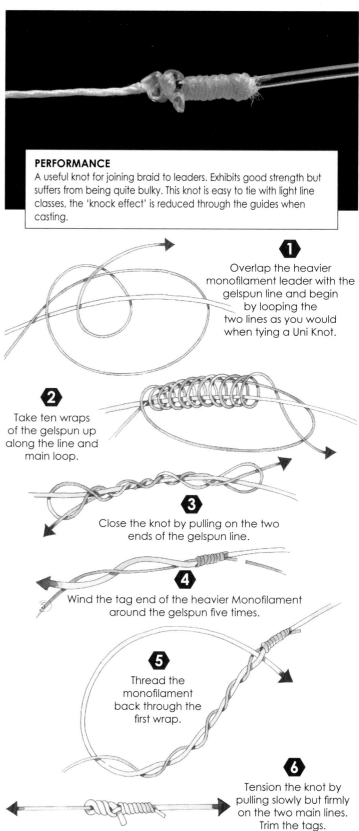

PERFORMANCE

A useful knot for joining braid to leaders. Exhibits good strength but suffers from being quite bulky. This knot is easy to tie with light line classes, the 'knock effect' is reduced through the guides when casting.

①

Overlap the heavier monofilament leader with the gelspun line and begin by looping the two lines as you would when tying a Uni Knot.

②

Take ten wraps of the gelspun up along the line and main loop.

③

Close the knot by pulling on the two ends of the gelspun line.

④

Wind the tag end of the heavier Monofilament around the gelspun five times.

⑤

Thread the monofilament back through the first wrap.

⑥

Tension the knot by pulling slowly but firmly on the two main lines. Trim the tags.

TED DONNELAN'S CONNECTION

This knot is best suited for attaching relatively light monofilament leaders to gelspun line and retains the full strength of the gelspun. It passes easily through the rod guides when casting and retrieving.

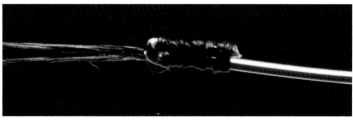

❶ Take the spliced end loop that you have tied in your gelspun with a Bimini Twist and the length of your leader that you have doubled to form a loop at one end. Pass the gelspun loop through the leader loop.

❷ Pull the tag ends of the leader through the gelspun loop.

❸ Then start threading the leader tags through the gelspun as shown and continue to complete 4 to 8 wraps as shown in diagram 4.

❹ The number of wraps will depend on the difference in the diameter of the two lines. The greater the difference in diameter between the two lines the fewer the wraps, and vice versa if the lines are closer in diameter.

❺ Tension the wraps by firstly applying pressure on both ends of the leader against the gelspun loop and then on the main length of the leader only.

❻ Pull the join up as tight as possible and then trim the shorter tag end of the leader.

DOUBLE BLOOD KNOT

We're often called upon to create leader or joining knots that combine lines of 'like' material. For example, top shotting the spool of a reel with braided line requires two lengths of braid to be connected. Anglers fishing with monofilament or fluorocarbon mainline material and wishing to join a length of heavier or lighter line of the same material require the services of a good knot. The knot we use most often in these circumstances is the Double Blood Knot. It is relatively easy to tie, maintains good strength and does not form an overly bulky knot. A Double Blood knot tied mid-spool and connecting two lengths of braid will form a strong compact knot that will not be noticed when casting and retrieving line. It's a great option when you lose half a spool of braid and need to top the reel back up.

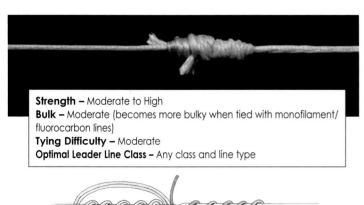

Strength – Moderate to High
Bulk – Moderate (becomes more bulky when tied with monofilament/fluorocarbon lines)
Tying Difficulty – Moderate
Optimal Leader Line Class – Any class and line type

CONNECTING BRAID TO SINGLE STRAND WIRE

A useful knot when targeting toothy fish that have no problems biting through the heaviest monofilament leaders.

PREPARE THE WIRE
Use a pair of pliers to double the wire back on itself and at the turned end form a turned eye like that on a hook.

BRAID TO SINGLE STRAND WIRE
Insert the tag end of the braid leader the same as you would on a Reverse Albright Knot.
Make 7 wraps back over both strands of wire and the braid leader towards the turned eye section of the wire. Secure the tag end of the leader under the central leader closest to the turned eye section and tighten up so that the wraps pull up tight on the braid tag and the wire eye. Trim the tag.

BRAID TO SINGLE STRAND WIRE
The procedure is like the mono knot above but with braid you should double it and do double the number of wraps as was done with the mono. At least twelve wraps should be used.
Trim the tags.

CHAPTER 2 BRAID DOUBLES

PLAITING A DOUBLE

Plaiting a double takes some effort, practice and time, and as such isn't a quick double used by many sports fishermen. It retains 100% of the original lines breaking strain.

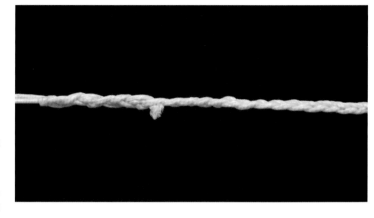

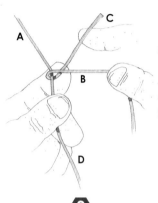

1 Measure off just over twice the length of line your finished double will be. Say our double will finish up at 4.5 metres, then you will need to double 9 metres of line plus half a metre or so for your tag. The main line or standing part is **A**. The returning length is **B**, and the tag is **C**. Let's call the loop formed, **D**.

2 As with the Bimini, your rod should be firmly in a rod holder and the clutch of the reel set on strike drag. Keeping the line tight by pulling away from your rod and reel, pass **C** over **B** (alongside **A**). Pull **B** tight. Because tension must be maintained throughout the plaiting process, it helps to wrap each successive leg in turn, around your fingers as shown.

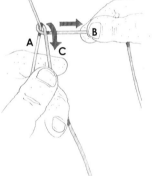

3 Pass **A** over **C** and pull **C** tight.

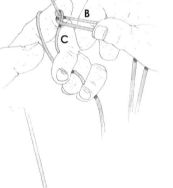

4 Pass **B** over **A** and pull **A** tight.

5 Pass **C** over **B** and pull **C** tight. Having completed the first cycle of the plait, increase tension on the line, even though some distorting may appear at the beginning of the plait. This is normal.

6 Now you are getting the idea, **A** goes over **C** then **C** is pulled tight. Always pull the leg you have just crossed really tight against the line coming from your rod and reel. That way your plait will be nice and firm.

7 Having plaited for at least a dozen cycles, or what appears to be far enough say 5 cm for 10 kg, 8 cm for 15 kg, 12 cm for 24 kg and so on, double the tag over to form loop **E** as shown.

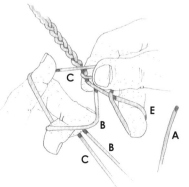

8 Loop **E** is plaited in just like the other two single legs. Secure the loop against the plait with the thumb and forfinger of the right hand as shown.

9

Transfer loop **E** to the index finger of your left hand and cross the leg **B** over it to the centre. Now pull **E** tight.

10

Pass **A** over **B**, pull tight.

11

Pass **E** over **A**, pull **A** tight.

12

B goes over **E**, pull **E** tight.

13

A has already gone over **B**, shown is **E** over **A**.

14

Shown is **A** over **B**.

15

Continue for one complete cycle of the plait then pass loop **D** through loop **C**.

16

Then pull the entire double through.

17

Secure the double by pulling on loop **D** against tag **C** to form a collar around the double.

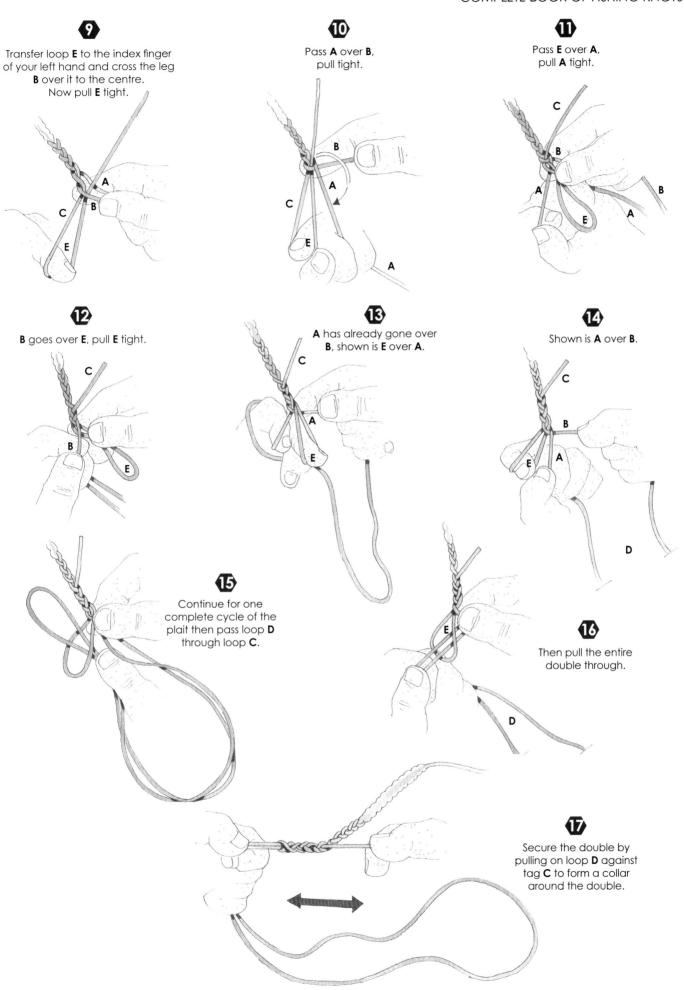

HARRO'S QUICKIE DOUBLE

This double is super quick to tie and is simply a multi turn overhand knot.

1 Double the length of gelspun line so that the doubled section is about 10cm longer than the required loop size.

2 Form a loop with the doubled line to just above the tag end.

3 Make a four turn overhand knot and pull tight smoothly.

BIMINI TWIST

This is a proven and extremely popular knot for creating doubles or loops in your main line for braid, gelspun or monofilament. It retains its full un-knotted lines strength. Every sportfisher who chases big fish should learn this knot.

1 Double over the braid and create a loop using 25 to 30 cm of line.

Pinch the lines and create 25 to 30 wraps in the loop.

2 You need to secure the loop and usually it's best to put it over your foot. Once the line is over your foot hold the main line in your left hand and the tag end in your right, both out at a 45 degree angle.

3 Place your index finger under the twists and pull back towards yourself until they become taught (as seen in the picture).

4 Angle the tag end along the loop while still pulling back with your index finger and the line will wrap itself around the already created twists, all the way to the start of the main loop.

5 Pinch the wraps and make a half hitch over one arm of the loop to lock the knot.

6 Then create another half hitch over both arms of the loop and pull down tight.

7 To lock the bimini twist you need to create a half loop up against the bimini loop using the tag end of the braid.

8 Wrap the tag end of the braid around the bimini loop six times (back towards the bimini knot) while ensuring you are under the initial loop you created. Pull up tight to lock the knot.

CHAPTER 3

BRAID TO TERMINALS

THUMB KNOT

A fiddly knot to tie but strong when using medium to large hooks, attaching other terminal tackle or as a double loop.

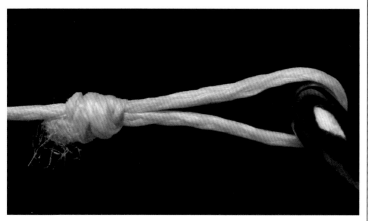

BRAID RING KNOT

Effectively this is simply a basic Blood Knot with more turns of the line to ensure the braid doesn't slip.

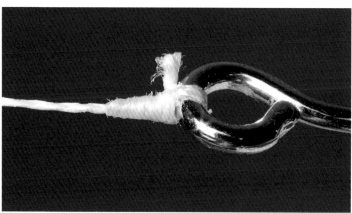

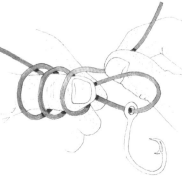

1
If you're attaching terminal tackle then thread with the line and make a loop. Pinch the loop crossover between your thumb and forefinger and commence wrapping the tag end of the line around your thumb, starting the wraps further up your thumb as shown. Make three wraps in total.

2
Thread the tag end of the line back up and under the thumb loops and away from the smaller loop. Secure the tag end with your thumb and middle finger.

3
Now grab the hook or loop and pull away from the thumb wraps until one wrap after another peel off your thumb.

4
Close and tighten the knot by pulling on the main line and tag, and the loop end. Trim tag.

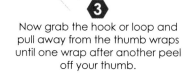

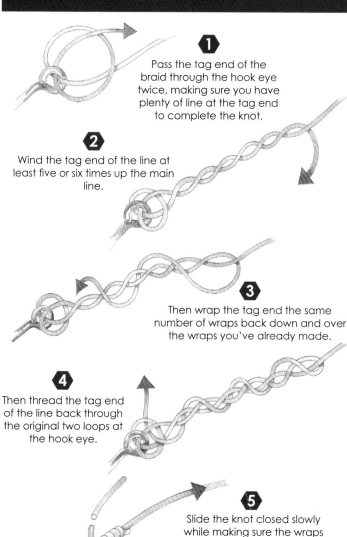

1
Pass the tag end of the braid through the hook eye twice, making sure you have plenty of line at the tag end to complete the knot.

2
Wind the tag end of the line at least five or six times up the main line.

3
Then wrap the tag end the same number of wraps back down and over the wraps you've already made.

4
Then thread the tag end of the line back through the original two loops at the hook eye.

5
Slide the knot closed slowly while making sure the wraps all lay down in sequence to prevent the knot bunching up on itself.
Trim the tag.

CHAPTER 4 | BRAID TO REEL

ATTACHING SUPER LINES TO REELS

This is the first step when setting up a reel for gelspun lines. Always wind the line onto the spool with moderate tension. If the knot tends to slide around the spool after tying, then you can use tape to hold it in position while starting the line winding process. If your spool does not have a Non-Slip braid core built in then strongly suggest to spool with 15-20 wraps of mono first, then attach braid with a suitable braid to mono knot.

1

Form a double loop around the arbour of the reel.

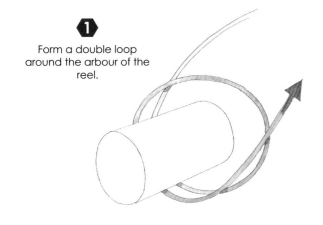

2

Commence by tying a Uni Knot around the main line.

3

Make at least double the number of wraps you would when using monofilament to avoid line slip. Twelve wraps are a good number.

4

Close the knot by pulling gently on the tag line to avoid bunching up the wraps as it locks down.

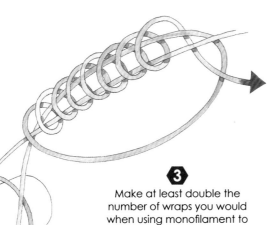

5

Slide the knot down fully and trim tag.

CHAPTER 5

BRAID TO BRAID

JOINING BRAID WITH DOUBLE UNI KNOT

This is a popular knot for joining lines of similar or different diameters.

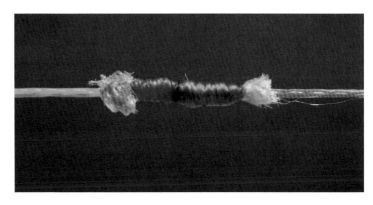

①

Overlap the two lines to be joined.

②

Wrap the double strand of line inside the formed loop.

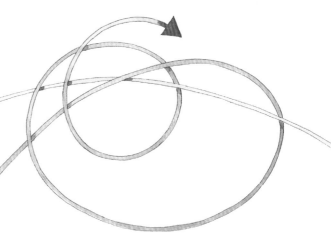

③

Make 4 – 6 wraps through the loop.

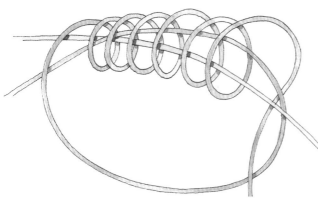

④

Close the first knot lightly, and then repeat the same knot with the other length of line.
Two knots will be formed in each line and around the other line.

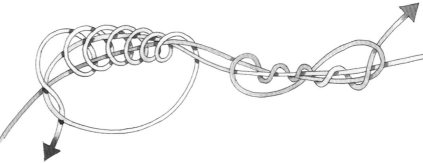

⑤

Close knots fully so that that snug up against each other and tighten each in turn.
Trim tags.

CHAPTER 6 MONOFILAMENT TO TERMINAL TACKLE

CENTAURI KNOT

A good knot for use with light lines and small swivels, hooks and rings. One of the simplest knots to tie. Requiring only 2 or 3 loops around the main line to successfully tie, means it can easily be tied in the dark.

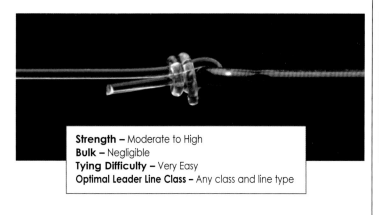

Strength – Moderate to High
Bulk – Negligible
Tying Difficulty – Very Easy
Optimal Leader Line Class – Any class and line type

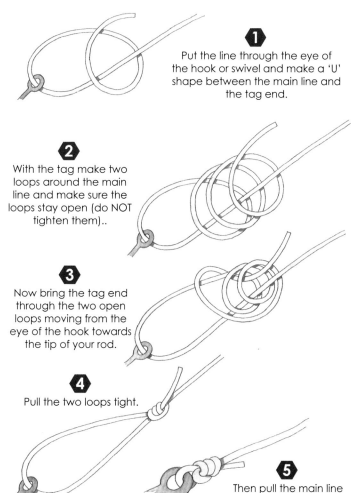

1 Put the line through the eye of the hook or swivel and make a 'U' shape between the main line and the tag end.

2 With the tag make two loops around the main line and make sure the loops stay open (do NOT tighten them)..

3 Now bring the tag end through the two open loops moving from the eye of the hook towards the tip of your rod.

4 Pull the two loops tight.

5 Then pull the main line so the knot will be tight against the eye of the hook. Cut the rest of the tag off.

PALOMAR KNOT

A very quick knot to tie and adequate in most fishing situations. It provides a simple means of attaching hooks, either to the end of your line or trace, or along your line as is the case when you're rigging a drop-shot for soft plastics.

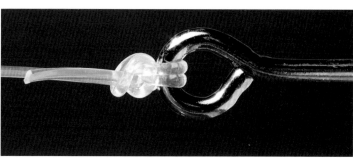

1 Double the leader and thread the loop end through the eye of the hook.

If you are using super lines, we suggest you make three passes through the hook at this stage to create the TRIPLE PALOMAR KNOT. Close the three loops at this stage before proceeding with knot.

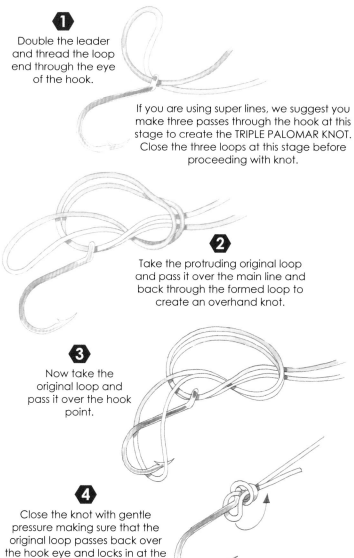

2 Take the protruding original loop and pass it over the main line and back through the formed loop to create an overhand knot.

3 Now take the original loop and pass it over the hook point.

4 Close the knot with gentle pressure making sure that the original loop passes back over the hook eye and locks in at the front of the knot. Trim tag.

LOCKED HALF BLOOD KNOT

A basic but very useful knot for attaching terminal tackle to line up to 15 kg breaking strain. Although it is better when used in much lighter lines. It is a good alternative knot from the Improved Half Blood Knot shown elsewhere.
It is a useful knot for attaching in-line spinners but loop knots are preferable for swimming lures requiring action.

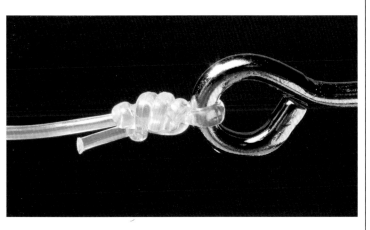

1 Thread the hook or swivel and take three to six wraps of the tag end up along the main line and then back through the first loop. The lighter the line the more twists, the heavier less.

2 Pinch the tag end and hook between your fingers and with your other hand start to pull the main line away from the hook so that the knot starts to close but not fully.

3 Now take the tag end of the line and thread it through the open loop that has begun to form at top of the knot.

4 Now close the knot up firmly and trim the tag.

HALF BLOOD KNOT

Many knots aren't suitable for attaching hooks when using extremely heavy monofilament. Too many loops simply make it almost impossible to lock a heavy mono knot up. This knot is strong and more than adequate for those purposes. The number of twists is determined by the breaking strain, lighter line more turns, heavier line less.

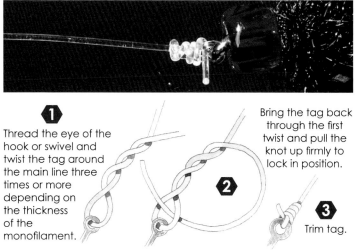

1 Thread the eye of the hook or swivel and twist the tag around the main line three times or more depending on the thickness of the monofilament.

Bring the tag back through the first twist and pull the knot up firmly to lock in position.

2

3 Trim tag.

IMPROVED BLOOD KNOT

This is one of the strongest knots for attaching a lure, jig head or hook to a line or leader up to about 15 or 20kg breaking strain when a tight (non-loop) connection is acceptable.

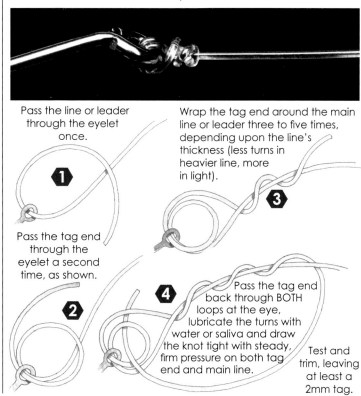

Pass the line or leader through the eyelet once.

1

Pass the tag end through the eyelet a second time, as shown.

2

Wrap the tag end around the main line or leader three to five times, depending upon the line's thickness (less turns in heavier line, more in light).

3

4 Pass the tag end back through BOTH loops at the eye, lubricate the turns with water or saliva and draw the knot tight with steady, firm pressure on both tag end and main line.

Test and trim, leaving at least a 2mm tag.

UNI KNOT

This is a widely used and easily tied knot for attaching terminal tackle such as hooks, swivels, rings, lures and flies to your line. It is suitable for lines up to around 15-20 kilograms breaking strain.

The knot can be tightened down fully to the terminal tackle or tightened to leave a loop as shown in figure 6.

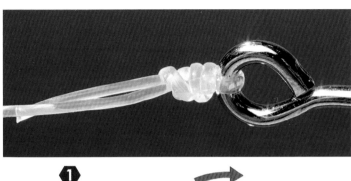

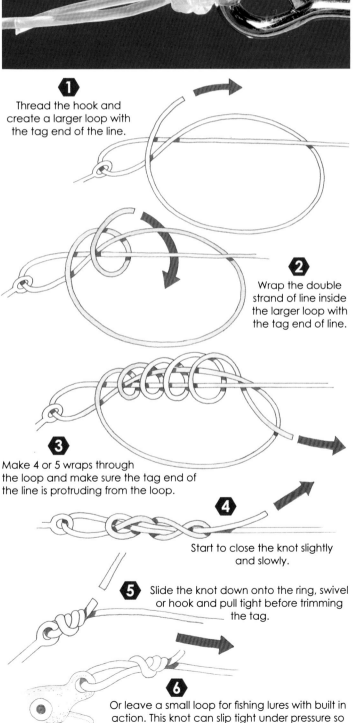

1 Thread the hook and create a larger loop with the tag end of the line.

2 Wrap the double strand of line inside the larger loop with the tag end of line.

3 Make 4 or 5 wraps through the loop and make sure the tag end of the line is protruding from the loop.

4 Start to close the knot slightly and slowly.

5 Slide the knot down onto the ring, swivel or hook and pull tight before trimming the tag.

6 Or leave a small loop for fishing lures with built in action. This knot can slip tight under pressure so checking occasionally when fishing will help.

CLINCH OR BLOOD KNOT

One of the most common and strongest knots for attaching medium sized hooks and other terminal tackle to line weights between 4 and 15 kg breaking strain.

It works best when attaching hook eyes and the like that have similar or less diameter than the line being used.

A Palomar or Uni Knot is more useful when attaching to thicker surfaces to avoid knot slip.

When using monofilaments under 20 kilograms breaking strain, make 5 turns. With heavier lines 2.5 turns are adequate.

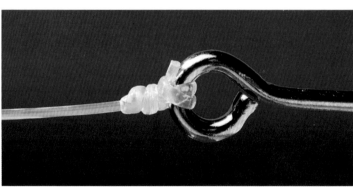

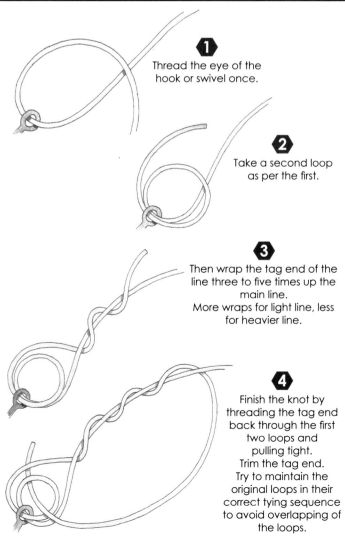

1 Thread the eye of the hook or swivel once.

2 Take a second loop as per the first.

3 Then wrap the tag end of the line three to five times up the main line. More wraps for light line, less for heavier line.

4 Finish the knot by threading the tag end back through the first two loops and pulling tight. Trim the tag end. Try to maintain the original loops in their correct tying sequence to avoid overlapping of the loops.

THUMB KNOT

A fiddly knot to tie but strong when using medium to large hooks, attaching other terminal tackle or as a double loop.

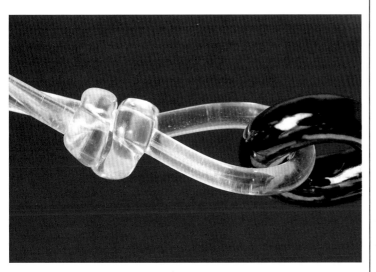

1

If you're attaching terminal tackle then thread with the line and make a loop. Pinch the loop crossover between your thumb and forefinger and commence wrapping the tag end of the line around your thumb, starting the wraps further up your thumb as shown. Make three wraps in total.

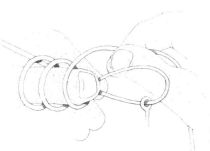

2

Thread the tag end of the line back up and under the thumb loops and away from the smaller loop. Secure the tag end with your thumb and middle finger.

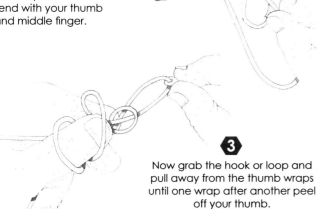

3

Now grab the hook or loop and pull away from the thumb wraps until one wrap after another peel off your thumb.

4

Close and tighten the knot by pulling on the main line and tag, and the loop end. Trim tag.

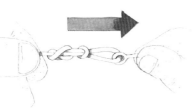

CATS PAW
(also known as an OFFSHORE KNOT)

This knot is used to secure offshore snap swivels to a double line. This is a neater knot than a Uni or Improved Clinch Knot.

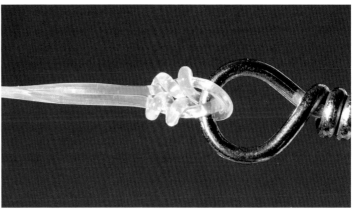

1

Pass the doubled over line through the eye of the swivel or hook. Twist the line and pass the swivel through the loop.

2

Then grasp the end of the loop and take it back up the double line by 80–100mm and hold the loop and the double section between your thumb and forefinger. Open the central loop above the swivel and pass the swivel up and through the middle opening from 3 to 8 times depending on the thickness of the line being used.

3

4

Take hold of the swivel with one hand and grasp the double main lines with the other and begin to pull from both ends to slowly draw down the wraps.

5

It's crucial to keep pressure on this knot while you tighten to make sure all the loops fall correctly into place and don't go over each other.

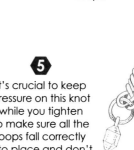

CHAPTER 7
MONOFILAMENT SNELLS

COMMON SNELL

A very useful knot for attaching up or down eyed hooks where it is important for the leader to be aligned with the hook shank. This is also a very important knot for constructing two hook rigs. When tying a Common Snell it isn't necessary for the leader to thread through the hook eye if it isn't necessary, either way is acceptable.

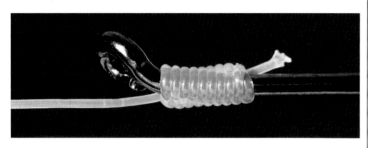

1
Thread the tag end of the leader through the eye or not depending on the hook type you are using. Form a loop along the shank of the hook.

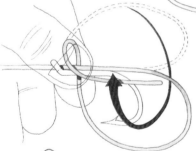

2
Pinch the line at the hook eye area and start wrapping the main loop back over the tag line and the hook shank.

3
After a few wraps the Snell will start to take shape.

4
Continue the wraps until you have the required number. More for light line, less for heavier line.

5
Pull the main line and the tag line in opposite directions so the knot forms tightly along the hook shank. Try and keep the Snell back from the hook eye a little to avoid cutting through from a rough hook eye.

6
Cut the tag.
If you're tying a two hook rig the tag end is used to tie another hook at the rear if required. If you intend to tie two hooks then allow enough of the tag line to do so.

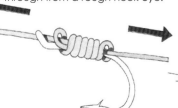

SIMPLE SNELL

A very quick and effective knot for attaching hooks or jigs. It does need both ends of the line to be free to tie this knot as both ends will need to be threaded through the hook eye.

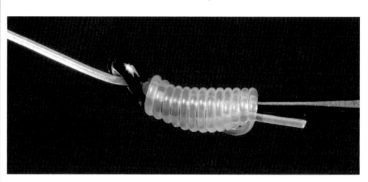

1
Take the shorter tag end of the piece of line and thread it through the hook eye from the underneath as shown.

2
Hold the shorter tag end back along the hook shank and overlap and wrap it with the longer main line snood.

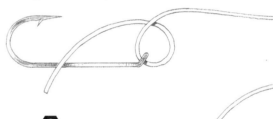

3
Perform at least 9 or 10 wraps with the snood (main) line and then thread the end back through the eye.

4
Trim the tag end and attach your snood to your fishing rig.

CHAPTER 8
MONOFILAMENT LOOPS TO LURES (AND HOOKS)

HARRO'S LOOP KNOT

A useful knot for attaching your leader to lure or fly. A variation of the Non-Slip Loop Knot that rates at over 90% breaking strain and forms a superior knot that tightens more easily.

A key with loop knots is to make sure that the loop you form is not so large as to foul up on trebles or lasso flies on the cast.

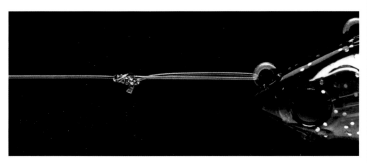

❶ Form an overhand knot in the line and pass the tag end through the eye of the hook.

❷ Take three or four warps with the tag end up around the main line above the overhand knot.

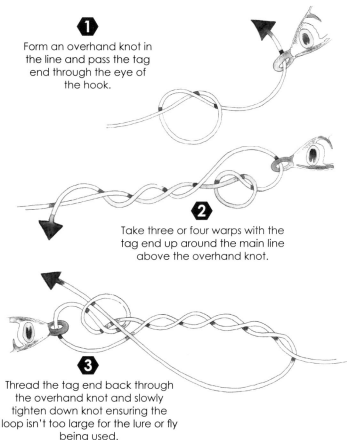

❸ Thread the tag end back through the overhand knot and slowly tighten down knot ensuring the loop isn't too large for the lure or fly being used.

❹ Trim the tag.

LOOP KNOT

An easy loop knot to tie and one that is very useful for those fishing lures such as hardbodies, surface swimmers and crankbaits.

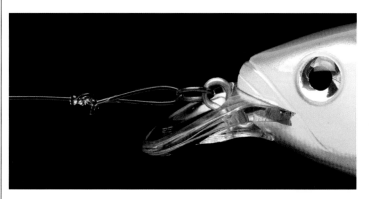

❶ Create a small overhand loop in the line leaving a tag end of 10 to 12 cm from this loop. Thread the tag through the tow point on the lure and then through the open overhand loop.

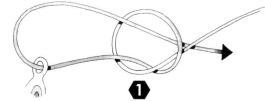

❷ Wrap the tag up the leader towards your rod tip, (7 times for light lines up to 8 lb, 5 times for 10 to 20 lb lines, 4 times for 30 to 50 lb line).

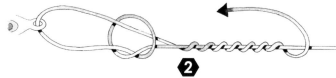

❸ Put the tag end back through the overhand loop that was initially created.

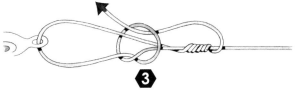

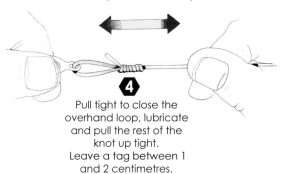

❹ Pull tight to close the overhand loop, lubricate and pull the rest of the knot up tight. Leave a tag between 1 and 2 centimetres.

LEFTY'S LOOP KNOT

Designed by Lefty Kreh to allow free swinging movement of a fly on the end of a tippet.
This small loop knot is easy to tie and retain a high proportion of the tippets breaking strain and is a useful loop connection for lure anglers using lines in the 8 – 30 kilogram category.

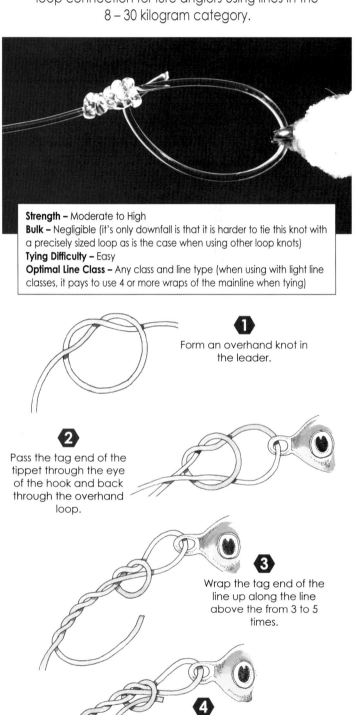

Strength – Moderate to High
Bulk – Negligible (it's only downfall is that it is harder to tie this knot with a precisely sized loop as is the case when using other loop knots)
Tying Difficulty – Easy
Optimal Line Class – Any class and line type (when using with light line classes, it pays to use 4 or more wraps of the mainline when tying)

1 Form an overhand knot in the leader.

2 Pass the tag end of the tippet through the eye of the hook and back through the overhand loop.

3 Wrap the tag end of the line up along the line above the from 3 to 5 times.

4 Thread the tag end of the line back through the original overhand knot.

5 Pull the knot tight using gentle pressure on the main line against the loop and trim the tag.

PERFECTION LOOP

A strong and relatively easy loop knot to use when you're using quite heavy leaders in relationship to your main line.

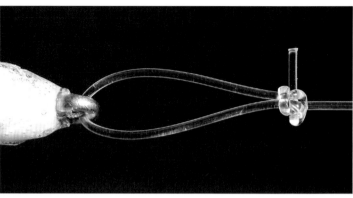

1 Tie an overhand knot in the leader and pass the tag end through the eye of the lure.

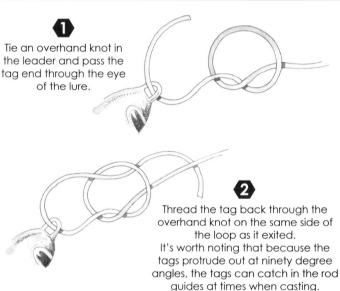

2 Thread the tag back through the overhand knot on the same side of the loop as it exited.
It's worth noting that because the tags protrude out at ninety degree angles, the tags can catch in the rod guides at times when casting.

3a (Standard Version) On the traditional tying of this loop the tag goes over the original loop and under the first internal loop. Then above the second internal loop and under the outer loop on the opposite side.

3b (Steve Starling adaption) On this version it is important for the tag to go over the original loop and under the two internal lines, then exits above the outer loop.

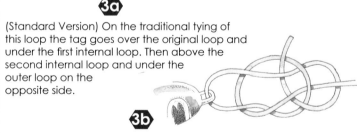

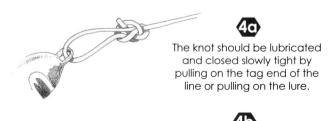

4a The knot should be lubricated and closed slowly tight by pulling on the tag end of the line or pulling on the lure.

4b Trim the tag.

HOMER RHODE LOOP KNOT

A useful knot for attaching heavier leaders when using lures with a strong swimming action.
It's an easy and quick knot to tie and is useful on heavy mono

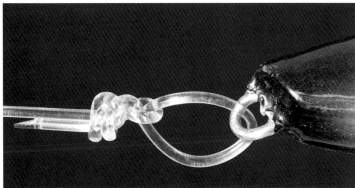

❶

Tie an overhead knot in the leader and then thread the tag end through the eye of the lure.
Then thread the tag end back through the overhand knot loop.

❷

Slide the formed knot down onto the eye of the lure by pulling on the tag end of the leader.

Tie a second knot by taking two loops back down the line and then threading the tag through the two loops formed.

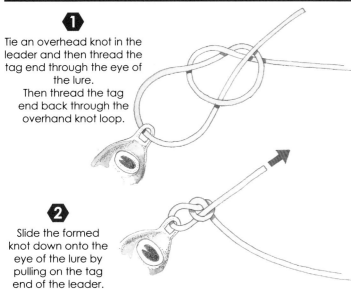

❸

❹

Close the second knot by again pulling on the tag end of the line.

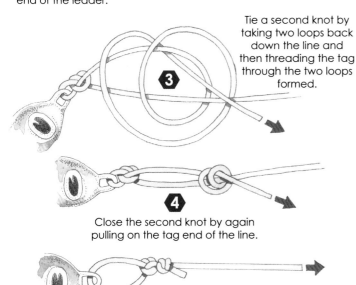

❺

Now pull on the main line until the two knots slide together and effectively lock the loop into an open position.
Trim the tag.

DUNCANS LOOP

This loop knot provides a fixed loop knot for attaching flies or lures to the leader.

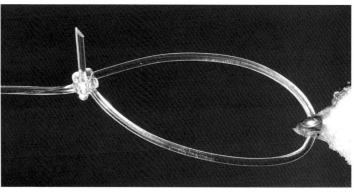

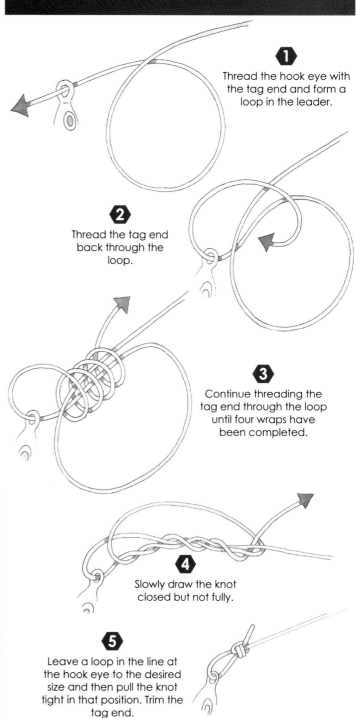

❶

Thread the hook eye with the tag end and form a loop in the leader.

❷

Thread the tag end back through the loop.

❸

Continue threading the tag end through the loop until four wraps have been completed.

❹

Slowly draw the knot closed but not fully.

❺

Leave a loop in the line at the hook eye to the desired size and then pull the knot tight in that position. Trim the tag end.

THE EASY LOOP KNOT

The Easy Loop was developed by Mick Caulfield and ticks off and some essential criteria.

Firstly it's fast, simple and easy to tie – even in low light or in the dark!

Secondly it is an adjustable loop, which means that you can adjust the actual length of the loop to suit the fishing conditions, lure type and desired action.

Lastly, and most importantly the knot configuration places the tag pointing back down the loop toward the lure. This drastically lessens the chance of catching and holding un-wanted's on the knot especially in weedy fishing situations.

PERFORMANCE

This knot also exhibits a very high percentage knot strength and it is suitable for both heavy and light leaders diameters. When pulled tight it won't slip and it can be adjusted to suit a particular loop length.

Most importantly it is a small profile footprint that keep bulk to a minimum and hence will increase bite liklehood.

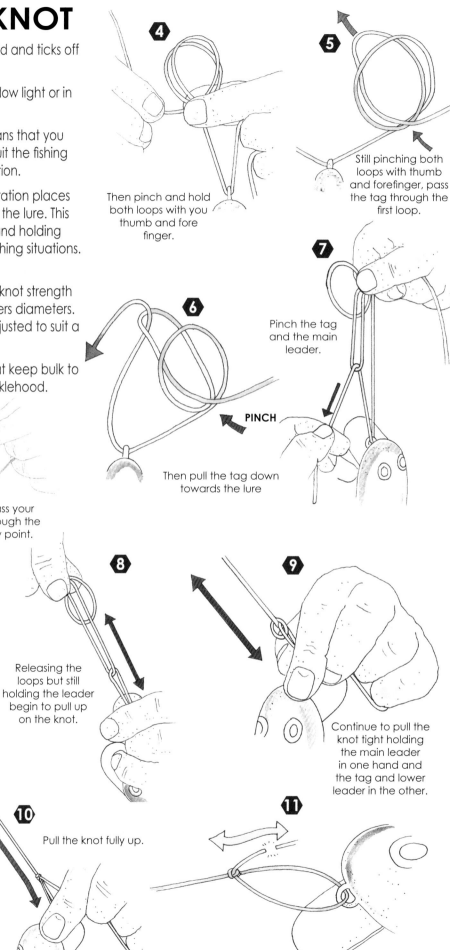

4 Then pinch and hold both loops with you thumb and fore finger.

5 Still pinching both loops with thumb and forefinger, pass the tag through the first loop.

6 **PINCH** Then pull the tag down towards the lure

7 Pinch the tag and the main leader.

8 Releasing the loops but still holding the leader begin to pull up on the knot.

9 Continue to pull the knot tight holding the main leader in one hand and the tag and lower leader in the other.

1 Simply pass your leader through the lure's tow point.

2 Form a simple loop and pinch and hold with your thumb and fore finger.

3 Simply form a second loop and place it through the first loop, so it sits behind the second loop.

10 Pull the knot fully up.

11

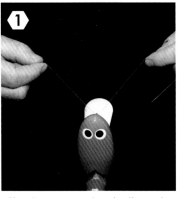

Simply pass your leader through the lure's tow point.

Form a simple loop and pinch and hold with your thumb and fore finger.

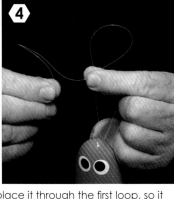

Simply form a second loop and place it through the first loop, so it protrudes behind.

Then pinch and hold both loops with you thumb and fore finger.

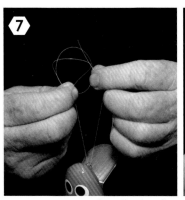

Pass the tag through the first loop.

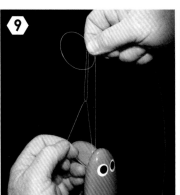

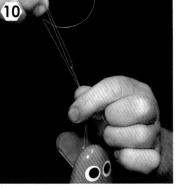

Pass the tag through the first loop.

Pinch the tag and the main leader.

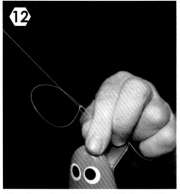

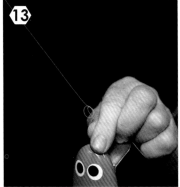

Releasing the loops but still holding the leader begin to pull up on the knot.

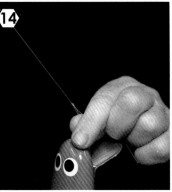

Continue to pull the knot tight holding the main leader in one hand and the tag and lower leader in the other.

Pull the knot fully up.

Pull the knot fully up.

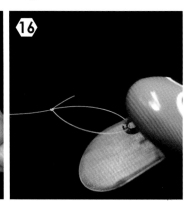

The completed knot. The loop can now be adjusted for length by simply pulling the tag with a pair of pliers. Then re tighten knot.

CHAPTER 9
MONOFILAMENT LOOPS

DOUBLE OVERHAND LOOP
(SURGEONS KNOT)

A very easy and effective loop knot to tie that offers a reasonably strong loop to the end of your line.
When this knot is tied with two separate lengths of line it is known as a Surgeons Knot, and is very useful for joining lengths of line and leaving one tag long as a dropper.

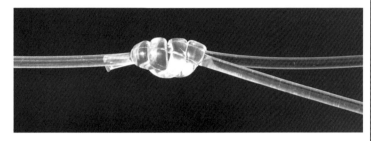

1

Double the line to form a flattened loop.

2

Take the loop and tie a largish overhand knot.

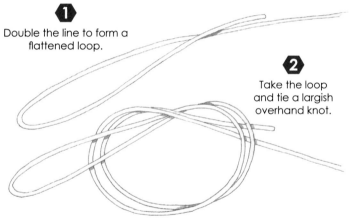

3

Take another pass through to create another wrap. On heavier lines this amount of wraps are fine, on lighter lines more (1 or 2) wraps are suggested.

4

Close the knot by pulling on both ends. Trim the tag.

DROPPER LOOP

This knot is ideal for constructing a loop anywhere along a length of line for the attachment of a hook or dropper leader.

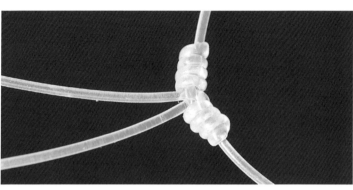

1

Make a large loop in the line where you require the dropper to be. Then pull through one section of the loop so that it crosses over the main line at one side creating a smaller loop.

Begin by twisting the smaller loop and creating more twists using your two index fingers.

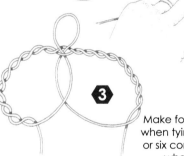

3

2

Make four complete twists (8 half twists) when tying the dropper in monofilament or six complete twists (twelve half twists) when tying the knot in gelspun.
Now thread the end of the larger loop through the small central loop that you have been twisting.

4

Take the threaded central loop and hang it over something firm that you can use for leverage. Pull gently on each trailing line to pull the knot up firmly to create the finished loop. When tying this loop in gelspun care should be taken not shear the line off either side of the knot.

5

The finished loop.

LOOP TO LOOP KNOT

A simple an effective method to join a fly line pre formed loop to a leader. It can also be used to quickly and easily join mono to braid.

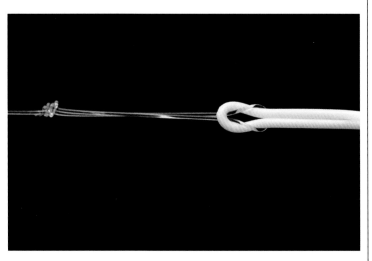

1

Insert the two loops together as shown.

2

Take one of the lines and thread it up and through the loop in the other line to join them.

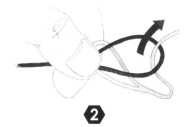

3

Now take that same line and thread it through a second time as shown.

4

Pull both ends of the lines so that the loops slide up snuggly together without hitching over.

LOOP AND CROSS LOOP CONNECTION

This knot will help eliminate the loop slipping and the lines cutting each other when using braid to braid connections, or braid to monofilament loop to loop connections.
It adds another interlock into the system to stop this slipping and cutting.

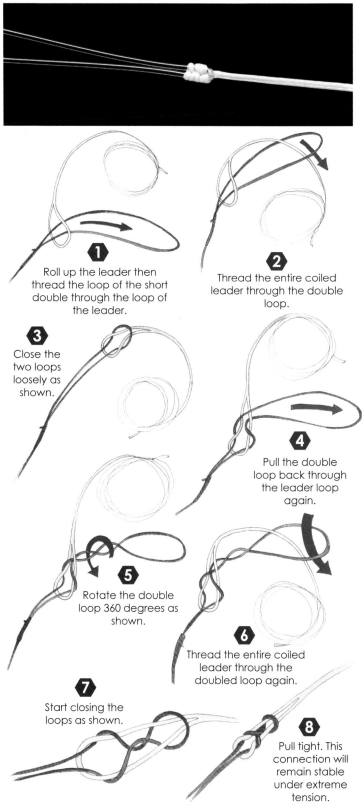

1
Roll up the leader then thread the loop of the short double through the loop of the leader.

2
Thread the entire coiled leader through the double loop.

3
Close the two loops loosely as shown.

4
Pull the double loop back through the leader loop again.

5
Rotate the double loop 360 degrees as shown.

6
Thread the entire coiled leader through the doubled loop again.

7
Start closing the loops as shown.

8
Pull tight. This connection will remain stable under extreme tension.

CHAPTER 10
MONOFILAMENT LINE TO LINE

DOUBLE UNI KNOT

This is a relatively easy knot to tie and is used for joining lines of similar or different diameters. It holds very well and is best used for lighter lines up to 12–15 kilograms breaking strain. It cast through the rod guides very nicely which makes for greater accuracy. When trimming the tags on this knot, cut them closely but leave a small tag to prevent the knot slipping. This knot is sometimes known as a Grinner Knot.

PERFORMANCE
A solid and useful knot but somewhat on the bulky side due to the full 5–6 wraps on the mono leader side of the knot. Suggest Kanelt is a better option.
The efficiency of this knot decreases as the diameter of the mono leader increases and the diameter of braid to leader becomes disproportionate.

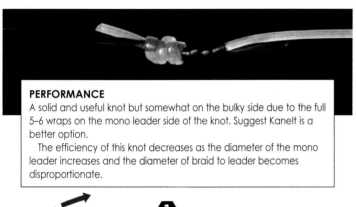

1 Overlap the leader with the braid (or main line) in a backhand loop and pinch the with fingers where the two lines overlap.

Start wrapping the tag end of the braid (or main line) through the previously created loop.

2 Wrap the tag end through the loop at least five times with mono but up to 10 times with light braid (around 4 lb strain) and 7 to 10 times with heavier (20 lb) braid.

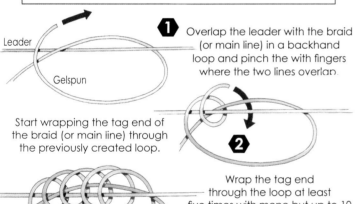

3

4 Close the knot by drawing smoothly on the tag end, but don't fully tighten this knot. Then take the tag end of the leader and repeat steps 2 and 3 until there are two similar knots formed.

Close the second knot slightly. Take the two tag ends of the knots and pull away from each other so that the two knots close and tighten on the line and slide up to each other. Make sure both knots tighten neatly against the line and each other.

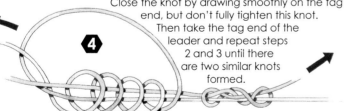

5

6 Trim the two tag ends.

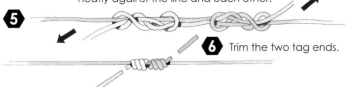

DOUBLE CENTAURI KNOT

This is a good knot for joining two lengths of line and retaining a strong breaking strength. It performs best when both lines are of a similar diameter but it can be used when there is a reasonable difference as well.

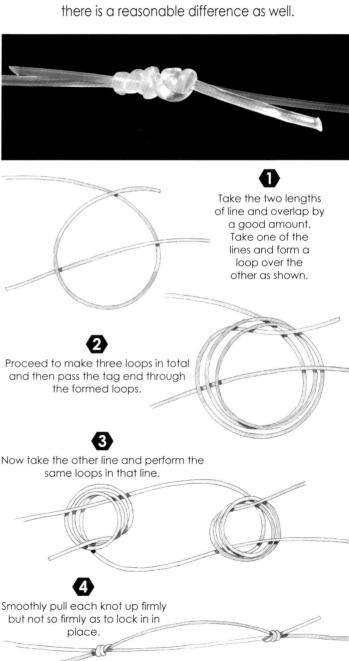

1 Take the two lengths of line and overlap by a good amount. Take one of the lines and form a loop over the other as shown.

2 Proceed to make three loops in total and then pass the tag end through the formed loops.

3 Now take the other line and perform the same loops in that line.

4 Smoothly pull each knot up firmly but not so firmly as to lock in in place.

5 Slide both knots together so they are snug and then tighten each knot separately. Then snug them together fully and locked each knot completely. Trim tags.

FULL BLOOD KNOT
or DOUBLE FOUR-FOLD BLOOD KNOT

This knot is most often used by fly fishers joining similar diameter lengths of monofilament or fluorocarbon when adding a tippet or constructing a tapered leader.
It is a neat and easy to tie knot and retains a good amount of the original breaking strain.
It is not suitable for joining widely dissimilar diameter lines.
It can be used for joining braid, gelspun and monofilament lines.
It's worth noting that because the tags protrude out at ninety degree angles, the tags can catch in the rod guides at times when casting.

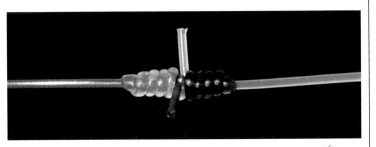

❶

Overlap the two lengths of line and start twisting both tag ends.

❷

Make 8 or 9 twists and then pass each tag through the central twist and in opposite directions.

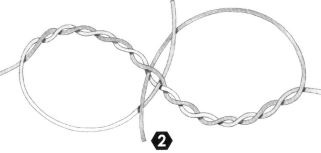

❸

Close the knot slowly with gentle tension on both ends of the twists, making sure the twists don't run back over on each other.

❹

Lubricate the knot and pull it firmly in place. Trim the tags.

IMPROVED FULL BLOOD KNOT

Used for joining two lines of quite different diameters. The doubling of the thinner line is the key to this knot.

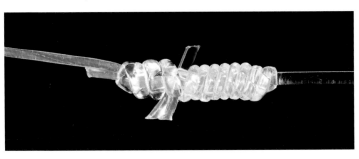

❶

Double the lighter line (braid or monofilament) and wrap over the heavier leader.

❷

Wind the doubled line up along the leader several times (at least four).

❸

Take the tag end of the heavier leader and pass it through the third or fourth wrap and then continue to wrap the thinner doubled line as in 2.

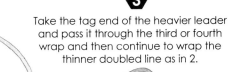

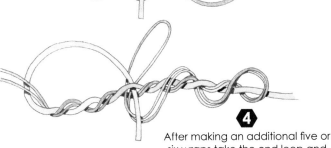

❹

After making an additional five or six wraps take the end loop and do two wraps back down the line and then pass it through the same wrap as the heavier tag but in the opposite direction.

❺

Close the knot slowly but firmly so that the knot forms evenly and no (non-tightened) sections are formed.

❻

Pull the knot up firmly and trim all tags.

REVERSE TWIST BLOOD KNOT

By doubling the wraps on this knot its strength is increased measurably. Instead of wrapping and coming straight back through the original loop the line is wound back over the original wraps as show.

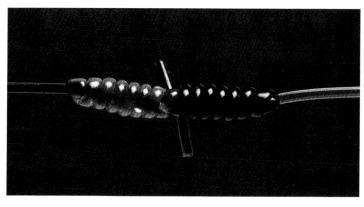

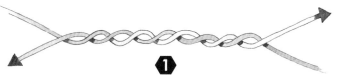

1

Take a good length of both lines and overlap them. Start twisting them together as shown.

2

Make four twist in one direction then four twists back over those loops in the reverse direction.

3

Thread the tag between the two lines at the first are they crossed as shown.

4

Do the same amount of outward and reverse wraps on the opposite side to the wraps.

5

Thread the tag end of those wraps back through the original central wrap but in the opposite direction to the first tag.

6

Slowly pull the main lines in opposite directions to close the knot and trim the tags.

CHAPTER 11 MONOFILAMENT LINE TO LEADER

ALBRIGHT KNOT

An easy knot to tie once performed a few times. This knot is perfect for sport fishing applications and retains relatively good knot strength. Its one big drawback is its tendency to slip and separate, often with an expensive in tow, after repeated casting. The heavier the line the more exaggerated and common is this slipping.

The tags facing forward tends to hit the rod guides and this continually knocking means the tag slips back through the original loop. Cutting the tags cleanly and not to close to the braid helps eliminate this as does only using this knot on light finesse lines when fishing for bream and trout etc.

1

Form a 'U' shape in the monofilament/fluorocarbon fishing line. Thread braid through top of 'U' and wrap line around tags and away from this point.

2

Wrap along monofilament seven times and then reverse wrap and begin cross-wrapping previous section.

3

Wrap braid back to starting point to provide a cross-wrap effect and pass braid tag through 'U' Shape in leader.

4

Lubricate and slowly draw knot tight.

5

Clip tag end extremely tight to braid as a loose tag will catch on guides during the casting process. Repeated 'catching' of the knot on rod guides when casting will loosen this knot and cause it to slip and fail.

REVERSE ALBRIGHT KNOT

This knot is a variation on the traditional Albright Knot. This version only effectively winds once up the line as opposed to both directions in the traditional tie. It is also possible to tie this knot with the main line braid or mono doubled.

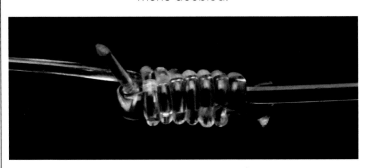

1

Take the mono leader and the braid and place them together as shown. Making sure you have enough line to complete the knot.

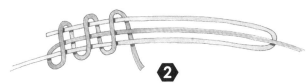

2

Double the mono leader back on itself at the knot end and pinch the tag end of the mono and the main leader length and the braid and start the wraps.

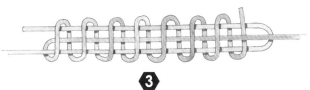

3

Keep wrapping the braid back towards main line as shown and continue to perform roughly 20 wraps ensuring that each is after the last and not overlapping.

After you've done 20 wraps take the tag (or tag ends through if mainline has been doubled) through the original leader loop as shown and start to draw the knot closed by holding the double leader ends and pulling on the tag(s) of the main line.

4

Draw the knot up as tight as possible and test a few times to make sure it's locked firmly. Trim the tags leaving about 2mm hanging.

SLIM BEAUTY

The Slim Beauty is an easy knot to tie that offers good strength, and casts well in most situations. It becomes difficult to tie only in very fine diameter lines, particularly where poor eyesight is an issue. This knot is ideal for most lure and bait fishing applications. It becomes an issue for anglers who are casting when leader knots are created using heavy line classes which become bulky; this tends to occur when tying a leader knot on line classes of 25 kg and larger. In the event that we plan to troll, jig or bait fish when using heavier leaders, rather than high speed casting, then the Slim Beauty is a great option despite the larger knot size.

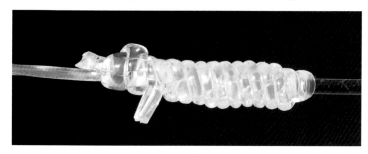

❶
Create looped double-hand knot.

❷
Slowly draw closed until a figure-of-eight forms.

❸
Thread the main line through the two loops of the figure of eight.
Then tighten the figure of eight

❹
Wind the main line around 6-8 times up the leader, then hold and start to wind back down to the figure of eight.

❺
Complete and wind the main line back 4-5 times to the figure of eight.

❻
Pass the main line through the first loop and carefully pull the knot up and finish.

SHOCK TIPPET AND LEADER KNOT

The strongest method for connecting a class tippet to a shock tippet without a double or Bimini Twist. It is also a very strong knot for joining a monofilament main line to a heavy leader.

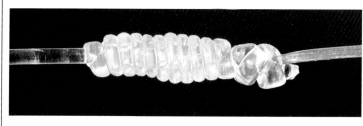

❶
Tie a double overhand knot in one end of your leader or shock tippet.

❷
Pull the overhand knot tight to the point where a figure of eight or double loop forms in the line.

❸
Thread the main line through the double loop as shown.

❹
Pull the double overhand knot in the heavier leader or shock tippet as tight as possible so that it flattens out as shown.

❺
Take a small hollow tube and lay it along the line as shown. Wrap the tube as shown and make eleven or twelve wraps.

❻
Then take the main line and thread it into the hollow tube so that the line is protruding out the other end of the tube and past the first wrap.

❼
Slowly slide the tube out from under the wraps making sure the coils don't unravel. This has formed a Nail Knot. Now close the Nail knot up but not so tight as to cut line.

❽
Once the join is closed trim the tags.

CHAPTER 12 MONOFILAMENT DOUBLES

HARRO'S QUICKIE DOUBLE

This double is super quick to tie and is simply a multi turn overhand knot.

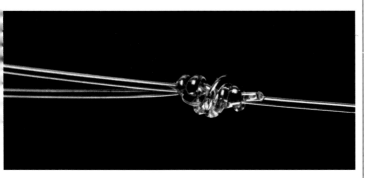

❶

Double the length of gelspun line so that the doubled section is about 10cm longer than the required loop size.

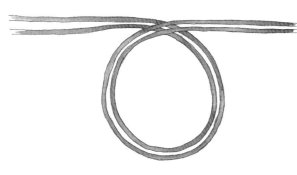

❷

Form a loop with the doubled line to just above the tag end.

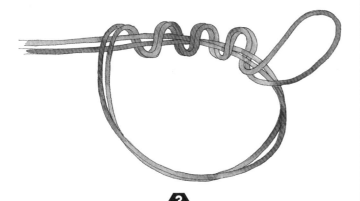

❸

Make a four turn overhand knot and pull tight smoothly.

SPIDER HITCH

A very easy double to tie, and an effective double for attaching small diameter lines to heavier lines. For high performance sportfishing however, it isn't as effective as doubles such as the Bimini Twist.

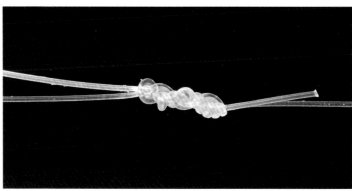

❶

Form a large loop in the main line and then form a smaller by overlapping the already double line. Pinch the second loop with your thumb and forefinger as shown.

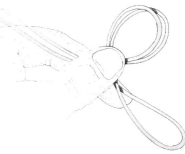

❷

Take the larger doubled loop and make five or six wraps over the thumb, starting further up the thumb and wrapping forward.
Pass the larger loop end through the smaller loop and draw the larger loop away from your thumb so that the knot forms as the loops pull off your thumb.

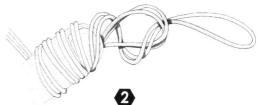

❸

Lubricate the loose knot and then tighten it by pulling the main line and the large loop in opposite directions until the knot pulls up tight. Trim the tag.

PLAITING A DOUBLE

Plaiting a double takes some effort, practice and time and as such isn't a quick double used by many sports fishermen. It retains 100% of the original lines breaking strain.

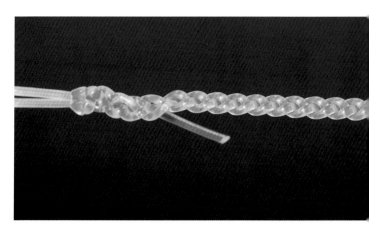

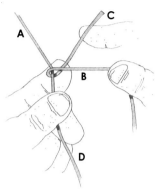

Measure off just over twice the length of line your finished double will be. Say our double will finish up at 4.5 metres, then you will need to double 9 metres of line plus half a metre or so for your tag. The main line or standing part is **A**. The returning length is **B**, and the tag is **C**. Let's call the loop formed, **D**.

2

As with the Bimini, your rod should be firmly in a rod holder and the clutch of the reel set on strike drag. Keeping the line tight by pulling away from your rod and reel, pass **C** over **B** (alongside **A**). Pull **B** tight. Because tension must be maintained throughout the plaiting process, it helps to wrap each successive leg in turn, around your fingers as shown.

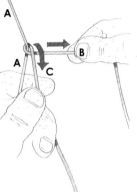

Pass **A** over **C** and pull **C** tight.

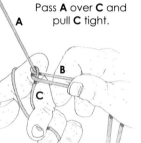

4

Pass **B** over **A** and pull **A** tight.

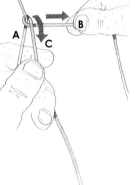

5

Pass **C** over **B** and pull **C** tight. Having completed the first cycle of the plait, increase tension on the line, even though some distorting may appear at the beginning of the plait. This is normal.

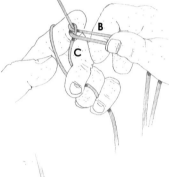

6

Now you are getting the idea, **A** goes over **C** then **C** is pulled tight. Always pull the leg you have just crossed really tight against the line coming from your rod and reel. That way your plait will be nice and firm.

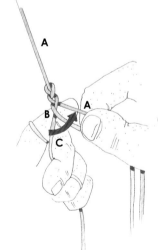

7

Having plaited for at least a dozen cycles, or what appears to be far enough say 5 cm for 10 kg, 8 cm for 15 kg, 12 cm for 24 kg and so on, double the tag over to form loop **E** as shown.

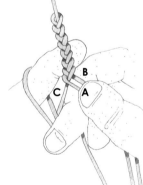

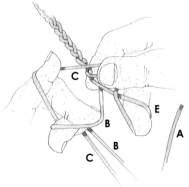

8

Loop **E** is plaited in just like the other two single legs. Secure the loop against the plait with the thumb and forfinger of the right hand as shown.

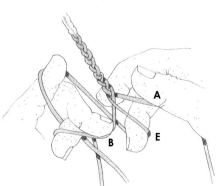

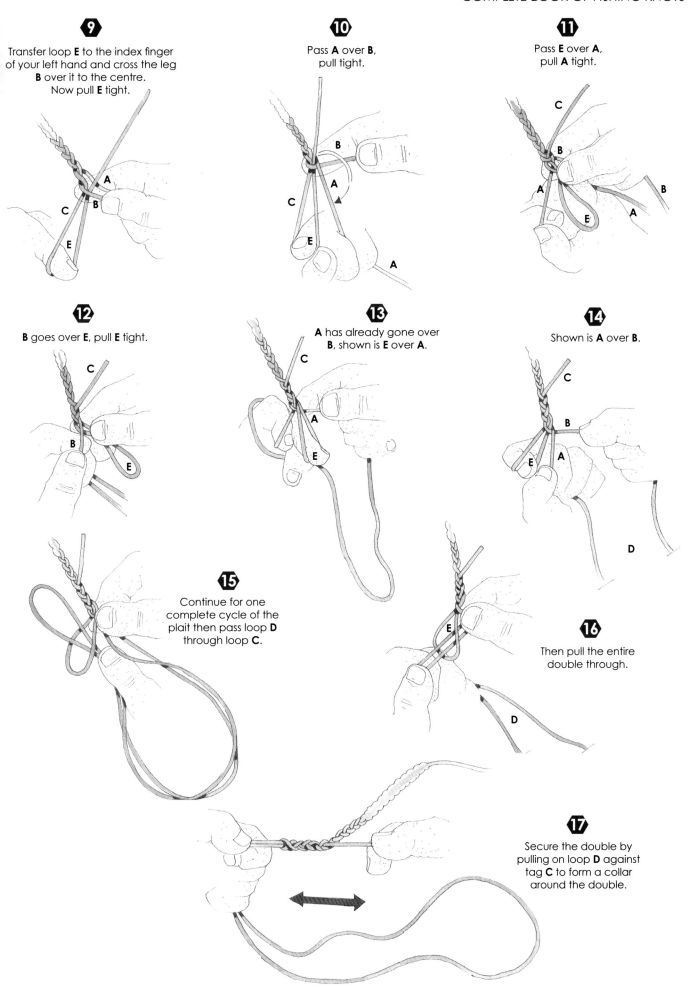

9
Transfer loop **E** to the index finger of your left hand and cross the leg **B** over it to the centre. Now pull **E** tight.

10
Pass **A** over **B**, pull tight.

11
Pass **E** over **A**, pull **A** tight.

12
B goes over **E**, pull **E** tight.

13
A has already gone over **B**, shown is **E** over **A**.

14
Shown is **A** over **B**.

15
Continue for one complete cycle of the plait then pass loop **D** through loop **C**.

16
Then pull the entire double through.

17
Secure the double by pulling on loop **D** against tag **C** to form a collar around the double.

BIMINI TWIST

This is a proven and extremely popular knot for creating doubles or loops in your main line for braid, gelspun or monofilament. It retains its full un-knotted lines strength. Every sportfisher who chases big fish should learn this knot.

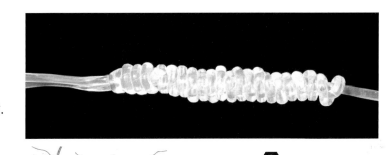

1 Double over the braid and create a loop using 25 to 30 cm of line.

Pinch the lines and create 25 to 30 wraps in the loop.

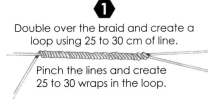

2 You need to secure the loop and usually it's best to put it over your foot. Once the line is over your foot hold the main line in your left hand and the tag end in your right, both out at a 45 degree angle.

3 Place your index finger under the twists and pull back towards yourself until they become taught (as seen in the picture).

4 Angle the tag end along the loop while still pulling back with your index finger and the line will wrap itself around the already created twists, all the way to the start of the main loop.

5 Pinch the wraps and make a half hitch over one arm of the loop to lock the knot.

6 Then create another half hitch over both arms of the loop and pull down tight.

7 To lock the bimini twist you need to create a half loop up against the bimini loop using the tag end of the braid.

8 Wrap the tag end of the braid around the bimini loop six times (back towards the bimini knot) while ensuring you are under the initial loop you created. Pull up tight to lock the knot.

THUMB KNOT

A fiddly knot to tie, but strong in medium classes. The loop formed here will pull up on itself under pressure.

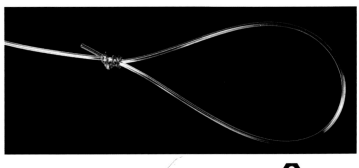

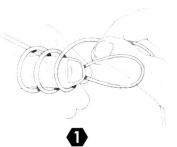

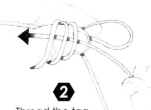

1 If you're attaching terminal tackle then thread with the line and make a loop. Pinch the loop crossover between your thumb and forefinger and commence wrapping the tag end of the line around your thumb, starting the wraps further up your thumb as shown. Make three wraps in total.

2 Thread the tag end of the line back up and under the thumb loops and away from the smaller loop. Secure the tag end with your thumb and middle finger.

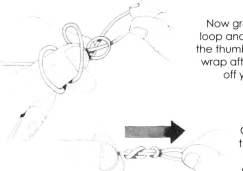

3 Now grab the hook or loop and pull away from the thumb wraps until one wrap after another peel off your thumb.

4 Close and tighten the knot by pulling on the main line and tag, and the loop end. Trim tag.

FISH COOLER DELUXE RANGE

Keep your catch
ICE COOL for LONGER

Small	915 mm x 460 mm x 300 mm	AC1136
Medium	1220 mm x 510 mm x 300 mm	AC1143
Large	1520 mm x 510 mm x 300 mm	AC1150
Extra Large	1830 mm x 510 mm x 300 mm	AC1167

Small

Medium

Large

Extra Large

KAYAK COOLER DELUXE RANGE

Medium	610 mm length - Top width 180mm - Bottom width x 400 mm	AC1112-11000
Large	910 mm length - Top width 250mm - Bottom width x 510 mm	AC1129-13700

Medium
With rubber handle

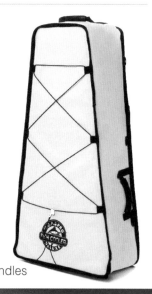

Large
With 3 rubber handles